CW00347497

THE BIG BOOK OF CAR TRIVIA

More than 1,200 amazing facts and funny stories

Simon Heptinstall

This book is dedicated to my
2001 Volvo S40 2.0

Which was made in the former Daf factory in
Nedcar in the Netherlands
This was a joint venture between Volvo and Mitsubishi
Mitsubishi built the Carisma range at the same plant at the
same time using the same platform
The Volvo was priced 50% higher than the Carisma
The S40 was the first car to earn a four-star
Euro-NCAP safety rating
My S40 is fading maroon colour that was originally
marketed as 'Torch Red Metallic'
Volvo means 'I roll' in Latin

Chapter one
From art on an Audi... to the 20lb satnav

1

A father visiting an Audi showroom was horrified when he eventually realised that his three-year-old daughter had wandered off ... and was scratching pictures on all the shiny new cars with a rock. The man was sued by the Chinese dealership for damage to ten brand new cars. He was forced to pay £7,600 ($9,500) in damages.

2

During the 2020/21 global coronavirus pandemic, medical researchers found that the average car steering wheel is home to more than 3,826 bacteria per square inch... that's 19 times more bacteria cells than the average toilet seat.

3

On average 150 drivers ask Google every month: 'How do I open a Ford Focus bonnet?'

4

German racing driver Ernst Loof holds a Formula One record from 1953 that is unlikely to be ever broken. Loof competed in just one F1 race: the German Grand Prix at the Nurburgring. Loof's Veritas car scored no points after he started the race but suffered a fuel pump failure. His racing car stopped after just two meters (six feet)... giving Loof the shortest-ever F1 career.

5

Research by Oxford University scientists has showed that pigeons follow the route of motorways in order to navigate their way home. The birds even make their aerial turns above motorway junctions.

6

You may not have heard of Scottish car manufacturer Galloway, which operated in the 1920s – but it was unique in motoring history.

The company was run by trained draftswoman and keen racing driver Dorothee Pullinger. Her factory was almost entirely staffed by women and Galloway cars were advertised as "a car made by ladies for others of their sex."

7

In 2006 the SSC Ultimate Aero TT set a new record for America's fastest supercar. It clocked 256.1mph (412kph) on a closed road in Washington State... with Chuck Bigelow, aged 70, at the wheel.

8

The world's first parking meter was installed in July 1935 in Oklahoma City, USA. Within a few weeks the surprising first motorist arrested for non-payment at the meter was Reverend C.H. North of the city's Pentecostal Church.

The Reverend later told his local court that he had gone to a shop to get change for the meter – the first use of a now very familiar excuse – and the judge dismissed the case.

9

Eccentric Italian soccer star Mario Balotelli crashed his Audi R8 supercar on the way to training at Manchester City. When police arrived and asked why he had £5,000 in cash on the passenger seat he said: "Because I am rich."

10

The first properly arranged race between two motorised road vehicles took place in Ashton-under-Lyne, Manchester, England in 1867. Two steam-powered carriages competed over an eight-mile course. The drivers however have not been recorded... they remained anonymous because they were both breaking the law by not being preceded by a footman waving a red flag.

11

A global supercar launch broadcast online in 2020 featured a high-tech film involving coloured lasers gradually revealing the car on stage with futuristic video backdrops. The big-budget movie took an expert team 1,000 studio hours and was targeted at an audience of millions.

The car? It was the Lego Lamborghini Sian. The 1:8-scale lime green vehicle came with working lights, paddle-shifter, monogrammed headrests and scissor doors. It involved almost 4,000 Lego Technic bricks… and cost $380/£350.

12

During the 2020/21 coronavirus lockdown in the UK the Ford Fiesta was overtaken as the UK's top selling car… by the Little Tikes Cozy Coupe, a bright red and yellow plastic push-along car for toddlers costing just £59.99.

13

The entire bodywork of American YouTube star Jojo Siwa's car – a Tesla Model X – is covered with 5,000 colour photographs of her own face.

14

German racing driver Erwin Bauer was tragically killed at the end of a 620-mile/1000km World Sports Car Championship race at Nurburgring in 1958. The 45-year-old drove a Ferrari 250TR to a creditable 10th place but didn't notice the chequered flag. He thought he had another lap to go. Bauer carried on racing at full speed when everyone else was gently cooling down. He raced up behind a slowing car, tried to overtake on a turn, lost control and fatally crashed into trees.

15

In June 1896 Henry Ford tried to drive his first car, called The Quadricycle, out of the small workshop behind his house in Detroit, USA for the first time. The Quadricycle had no body - it was little more than wheels, a seat and an engine. Nevertheless Ford had miscalculated the width. It wouldn't fit out through his workshop door. The great automotive pioneer had to use an axe to chop the door opening wider to get his Quadricycle out on to the road.

16

Britain's worst ever traffic jam stretched for 41 miles along the M6 in Lancashire in April 1987. It was estimated that around 200,000 people and 50,000 vehicles were stuck in it.

17 - 23

How to escape a car hanging off the edge of a cliff (From artofmanliness.com)

1) If the car is sliding, execute these steps quickly but smoothly.
2) Escape through front doors if over solid ground. Use window if opening door might shift weight dangerously.
3) If front hanging over cliff, set parking brake to lock rear wheels, turn off engine, unbuckle seatbelt.
4) Gently shift moveable weighty items, like bags, into back seat.
5) Slowly recline your seat and slide into back of vehicle.
6) Exit through back door.

24

The largest roundabout in the world is believed to be in Putrajaya, Malaysia. Its diameter is 2.7 miles (3.5km).

25

In 1981 Honda introduced the Electro Gyro-Cator - the first commercially available car navigation system. The 20lb (9kg) unit featured a map display mounted on top of the dashboard but was conceived in the days before access to GPS satellites for positioning information.

Instead, the Gyro-Cator used its helium gyroscope to try to track the distance and direction travelled from a defined start point. The option was available on the Honda Accord and cost $2,746... around a quarter of the cost of the car. It was a total flop and was withdrawn the following the year.

Chapter two
From tiny American cars...
To John Lennon in an Austin Maxi

26

American Austin was a company formed to market the rather small British Austin 7 to Americans in the thirties. Parts were shipped to America and assembled in Butler, Pennsylvania from 1930. It boasted 40mpg and was advertised as: "A car for the tiny open spaces." Unfortunately the Great Depression and American taste for big cars conspired against the 'tiny' concept. Within four years American Austin sales had plummeted and the company went bankrupt.

27

A young British couple were forced to spend their wedding night repeatedly driving around London's orbital road, the M25, in a bus. In 1991 Sue and Chris Glazier won a mystery tour in a radio station competition and were told they would be travelling at 50mph (80kph) all night.

"My wife thought it would be the Orient Express," said Chris. In fact the radio station had arranged a wedding reception at the unromantic Thurrock Service Station, then made the couple board a specially chartered bus. They spent the whole night making laps of the 118-mile ring road before returning to the service station in the morning for a fried breakfast.

28

The first purpose-built petrol station opened in St Louis, Missouri, USA in 1905. Prior to that, car drivers always had to refuel at pharmacies.

29

Only the best and most experienced Audi technicians are allowed to work at the company's Neckarsulm factory in Germany, which builds the R8 supercar. The workers here are the company's longest-serving and best-performing employees and are nicknamed 'silver liners' - because most of them have been with Audi so long they now have grey hair.

30 – 38

Nine Chrysler advertising slogans through history

1988: *The one thing you always wanted in a luxury car: Everything*
1979: *Add a little life to your style*
1974: *You've always deserved this much car*
1968: *Make your move*
1960: *The car of your life for the time of your life*
1959: *The lion-hearted car that's every inch a new adventure*
1953: *America's first family of fine cars*
1938: *Chrysler sweeps on in the low-priced field*
1930: *A Chrysler in the family brings a joy all of its own*

39

Swashbuckling Canadian gentleman racer Captain John Duff
fought a famous 100-mile driving duel with John Parry-
Thomas at Brooklands circuit in 1924. He lost despite his
21-litre Blitzen Benz lapping at an impressive 114mph.
At the end of the race, however, Captain Duff's brakes failed
and he was unable to slow the car. He managed to continue
steering at full speed, leaving the circuit, careering over the
grass embankments, crashing through trees and eventually
coming to rest far from the circuit against a public telegraph
pole. Duff was unhurt… and later went on to become a
Hollywood stunt double for Gary Cooper.

40 - 42

A survey of UK motorists in 2019 found:

> - More than a quarter see their car as part of their personal image.
> - Drivers under 34 years old were more likely to be 'badge snobs'
> - 35% claim a flashier car impresses their friends.

43

As a warning to others, Spanish Guardia Civil released a photo of a Skoda Fabia submerged in beautiful turquoise Mediterranean Sea off the holiday island of Mallorca. It followed an incident in 2020 in which a 26-year-old man reached 125mph (200kph) in the Fabia and drove off a cliff, plunging far out into the sea. Amazingly he was unscathed... but when rescued was promptly charged with reckless driving.

44 - 52

Roadside car refuelling points are called:

- Gas or fuelling station (USA and most of Canada)
- Gas bar (Some of Canada)
- Petrol station (UK)
- Garage (UK, Ireland, Australia, New Zealand and South Africa)
- Servo (Parts of Australia)
- Service station (Australia, France, Italy, Japan and New Zealand)
- Fuel station (Israel)
- Gasoline stand or SS (Japan)
- Petrol pump or petrol bunk (India)

53

Millionaire rock star Noel Gallagher forgot he'd bought a pristine classic car for £110,000 ($136,000). The former Oasis guitarist was shocked when a beautifully restored 1967 Jaguar Mark II arrived at his house on a delivery truck. It turned out he had ordered it spontaneously two years previously. Since then a specialist company had been carefully restoring it for him.

At the time he ordered it he had hoped to soon learn to drive. But he had never got round it and forgot the whole thing. So he has never driven the classic car he forgot he bought... and it still sits unused in his garage.

54

Latest Scottish government statistics show men are 11 times more likely to be convicted of any driving offence than a woman.

55

Wild, long-haired American professional wrestler Chuck Palumbo (WWE tag team champion 2002) retired to work on TV... and became the most unlikely presenter of a Discovery Channel show about doing up old cars.

56

John Lennon passed his driving test late in 1965 when he was already 25. He borrowed a white two-door Triumph Herald Convertible owned by producer George Martin for the test and the other three band members gathered to congratulate him afterwards.

Lennon was never a confident driver though, despite once buying a psychedelically decorated Rolls Royce.

In 1969 the Beatle went on a driving holiday in a humble rented Austin Maxi in the Scottish Highlands with pregnant Yoko Ono and his son Julian. He somehow managed to drive into a ditch. They all needed hospital treatment – and that was the final straw for Lennon. He never drove again.

Chapter three

From a silent dragster...
To a 20,000-mile pub crawl

60

At Tuscon, Arizona, in 2020, racer Steve Huff took his
custom-built dragster to a quarter-mile time of just 7.52
seconds and a top speed of 201.07 mph. Huff's 2,400bhp
machine, called 'Current Technology', was the first
ELECTRIC dragster to break the 200mph barrier... so the
record run was done in total silence.

61

**Washing a car at home uses up to 20 times more water
than an automated car wash.**

62

In 2018 Aston Martin engineers built a one-off supercar to
perform at the Goodwood Festival of Speed... based on the
tiny Toyota iQ hatchback.
The mini city car was fitted with the enormous 4.7-litre V8
engine, rear-wheel drive and seven-speed semi-manual
gearbox, all from an Aston Martin Vantage. The little Toyota
proceeded to shock onlookers by accelerating from 0-62mph
in 4.2 seconds and hitting a top speed of 170mph (274kph).

63

Italy's Polizia used two black 1962 Ferrari 250 GTEs as police cars in Rome. The only adaptation was that the 143mph (230kph) two-door coupes were fitted with a flashing blue light on their roof.

Selected lucky police drivers were sent to Ferrari headquarters in Maranello for special training. One of the cars, however, was destroyed in a crash quite soon after.

The other surprisingly survived intact for six years on the force. After its turn of duty, it was carefully preserved and at the time of writing is for sale with a British Ferrari specialist for around $500,000/£410,000.

64

The "most satisfying car to own" in the UK isn't a supercar or luxury limo, according to a survey of 10,000 owners by motoring website honestjohn.co.uk. The winning vehicle was the humble Hyundai Ioniq, a five-door family hybrid hatchback from Korea.

65

In 1898 bowler-hatted businessman and automotive inventor Elwood Haynes astonished one of his earliest customers by delivering his pioneering horseless carriage personally.

This involved Haynes driving the spartan open-topped car single-handed from his workshop in Kokomo, Indiana, all the way to the customer's door in New York City, USA.

This amazing delivery job was the first 1,000-mile car journey ever completed in the United States.

66 - 76

The top 10 car movie scenes

(according to thesun.co.uk)

1) The Mini chase in 'The Italian Job'
2) Harry and Ron chasing the Hogwarts Express in a flying Ford Anglia in Harry Potter and the Chamber of Secrets
3) John Travolta singing Greased Lightning around the Ford Deluxe Convertible in Grease
4) The DeLorean leaves streams of fire as it travels through time in Back to the Future
5) Thelma and Louise drive off a cliff
6) The bus-hanging-off-a mountain-cliff scene in the Italian Job
7) Bruce Wayne driving a Lamborghini Murcielago through Gotham in the Dark Knight
8) Chitty Chitty Bang Bang flies for the first time
9) T-Rex attacks the jeeps in Jurassic Park
10) Bohemian Rhapsody singalong in Wayne's World

77

Portly British TV presenter Mike Brewer was approached to join BBC Top Gear as the replacement for Jeremy Clarkson in 2015. However Brewer opted to stay with his own show 'The Wheeler Dealer'.

78

McLaren offered an exclusive extra with the 2018 Speedtail. Buyers could specify the car's badge made from white gold and carbon-fibre by a craftsman in Birmingham Jewellery Quarter for an additional £50,000 ($61,000).

79

During filming of Fast & Furious 7 around £10 million ($12 million) worth of cars were destroyed in stunts. The 270 vehicles wrecked included three (a Dodge, Subaru and Camaro) that were dropped from a plane at 10,000ft with parachutes that failed to open.

80

Aston Martin was founded by two businessmen; but only one is remembered in the company name. Lionel Martin (partnered by Robert Bamford) launched Bamford & Martin in 1913. The brand was re-christened Aston Martin a year later – after Martin produced an impressive driving performance in time trail event called ASTON Hill Climb. Bamford's name was quietly dropped from the brand and has been largely forgotten.

81

Portuguese soccer player Christiano Ronaldo wrecked his brand new Ferrari 599 GTB after losing control on a patch of oil in a Manchester tunnel just two days after buying it in 2011. The footballer was trying his £200,000 ($250,000) car for the first time. He escaped unhurt but the car was written off.

- A French businessman bought the wrecked Ferrari for around £30,000 ($38,000)… then posted it for sale on eBay at £250,000 ($314,000).

82

Motor-mad staff at Motortrend.com have been pitting supercars against each other in an annual series of 'The World's Greatest Drag Race' since 2011.

The latest ¼-mile sprint between 12 high performance cars, at the runway at Vandenberg Air Base in California, included a Mustang Shelby GT350, Toyota GR Supra, Lamborghini Urus, Bentley Continental GT V8, Mercedes AMG GT 63S, McLaren Senna, Porsche 911, Aston Martin Superleggera and Dodge Challenger Hellcat Red Eye.

The winner? All the entrants were very close at the finish, apart from the McLaren Senna… which surprisingly destroyed the field, beating them all by more than a second.

83

Price and style were found to be no guarantee of reliability in a recent survey by What Car magazine.

It found that the most reliable used cars in the UK were the Lexus CT Hybrid, and more humble Suzuki Swift and Toyota Auris Hybrid.

The least reliable second-hand cars were the Audi A3 diesel, Ford Focus diesel and Vauxhall Zafira. Only 4% of Lexus CT owners reported any problem in the survey… and those were only minor battery issues.

84

Eccentric British adventurer Ben Coombs spent seven months driving his P-reg (1996) TVR Chimera from the world's most northerly pub (in Svalbard in the Arctic Circle) for 20,000 miles to the most southerly pub (in Tierra del Fuego, Chile).

Chapter four

From the hairiest car in the world…
To the 'passatwind'

85

According to the Guinness Book of Records the world's hairiest car is a Fiat 500 owned by Maria Mugno of Salerno in Italy. She has spent hundreds of hours importing bags of human hair from India, which she then glues onto every surface of the car, inside and out, including the steering wheel and doors. Her furry Fiat is still road-legal however and is a familiar sight being driven around Salerno regularly.

86

The 1956 Tour de Corse involved 24 hours of almost non-stop full speed driving on some of Europe's narrowest, twistiest mountain roads. A Renault Dauphine driven by Belgium's Gilberte Thirion won – the first major rally win for a woman.

87 - 97

A recent survey of UK drivers found that despite well publicised economic and environmental benefits, more than half (57%) were still reluctant to buy an electric car.

They were polled on the ten factors that would persuade them to change their minds. In order of importance, these were:

1) Quicker and more convenient charging
2) Having guaranteed lower running costs than a petrol/diesel car
3) Offering a confirmed range of at least 200 miles on a single charge
4) A battery that definitely lasts at least several years
5) A government grant towards the purchase
6) Everyone trusting in the technology
7) The driving performance must be as good as a traditional car
8) Definite assurance that they are helping the environment
9) The car must hold its value
10) The car's battery must be recyclable

98

Ettore Bugatti founded a rather famous specialist car company in 1909 in Molsheim in north-east France. But Ettore did not come from an engineering background, however, but from a family of artists. In fact, his father was a famous designer of arty jewellery.

99

In a recent stunt to promote the Bloodhound Project – an attempt to build a vehicle to break the land-speed-record using a Rolls Royce jet engine – an extraordinary race was held on a South African salt flat. Here's how it unfolded:

o The Bloodhound 'car' lined up alongside a standard (un-named) road car, a Bugatti Chiron and a Formula One car. It was a unique chance to see how their acceleration compared.

o Within seven seconds the F1 car was slightly ahead, having reached 162mph (261kph). The Bugatti was close behind, travelling at 140mph (225kph), while the standard car had reached just 56mph (90kph). The Bloodhound's jet was slow to pick up power, giving the others chance to build up a lead.

o After 12 seconds however the jet car was starting to catch up. The leading trio were surprisingly close, while the road car was beginning to be left behind.

o Suddenly, after 24 seconds, the race is effectively over. The Bloodhound's jet spools up to maximum power and it roars off, passing 370mph (595kph to leave the others in its huge trail of dust.

o The F1 car hits 203mph (327kph), Chiron 248mph (399kph) but the road car is not even showing in the video, back in the distance at just 98mph (158kph).

o Meanwhile the Bloodhound continued to show off, increasing speed to 630mph (1014kph)... and disappearing out of sight towards the horizon.

100

The fledgling BMW company boldly built its first car in 1929… under licence and the watchful eye of Britain's much larger and more established global name: the giant Austin car company. Sadly the Austin brand disappeared in 1987 while BMW is now one of the top 12 producers of cars in the world.

101-106
Five stories about Rolls Royce
(from Topgear.com)

- The Spirit of Ecstasy statuette fixed to the front of the car is valued so highly that there is a safe on the shop floor at the Goodwood factory containing only the number of mascots necessary for one day of production. The safe's code is known only by a small circle of craftspeople.

- Suspension testing of the Phantom Extended Wheelbase model involved far more rigorous testing than normal. At one point the car was hit with such a severe experimental knock that a seismometer was triggered 20 miles away from Goodwood, in Worthing, Sussex. The car, however, was fine.

- Wine experts advise that the optimum serving temperature of non-vintage Champagne is around six degrees centigrade and of vintage Champagnes is around 11 degrees centigrade. That's why Rolls-Royce equips its cars with a fridge that operates two cooling modes, chilling to six degrees and 11 degrees.

- Rolls Royce seat leather is sourced from only the finest bulls, reared at high-altitude to avoid blemishes caused by insect bites.

- While testing the drop-top Rolls-Royce Dawn, test analysis engineers were required to wear skimpy shorts so they were able to detect any drafts around their legs and feet.

107

Indian cricketing star Sachin Tendulkar is now a multi-millionaire with a collection of luxury cars, including a specially built BMW i8 and a Ferrari 360 given to him by Michael Schumacher. But the famously modest Tendulkar, the sport's highest-ever international run scorer, has also kept his first car to remind himself of his more humble roots. He still owns the tiny Maruti 800 hatchback he bought when he was 17 for just £600 ($750).

108 - 111

For some strange marketing reason, many of VW's cars were named after winds.

- ➢ The Golf referred to the Gulf Stream
- ➢ The Jetta to the Jet Stream
- ➢ Scirocco was named after a specific Saharan wind
- ➢ Passat derived from the 'passatwind' - German for tradewind.

Chapter five

From the Corvette's embarrassment…
To the world's fastest car

112

One of America's most iconic sports cars had a rather humiliating birth in 1953. The first few models of the Chevrolet Corvette had to be pushed off the end of the production line… because they wouldn't start.
Engineers had failed to note that the new fibreglass body wouldn't allow the grounding of the electrical system as a metal one had always done before.

113

Strangers often struggle to get into a TVR Tuscan Speed Six (1999-2006) sportscar. The doors were opened by pressing a 'secret' button no-one could ever find. It was hidden under the wing mirrors.

114

Motoring safety experts claim that drivers who sit higher feel as if they're driving slower. Researchers found that SUV drivers, who are piloting the vehicles most prone to roll, drive too fast but feel like they're crawling along. Experts advised lowering any driver's seat to give the sensation of more speed… without the need for really speeding.

115 - 135

Internet comparison site comparethemarket.com used hashtag analysis to find the most Instagrammed supercars.

The results were:

1) Lamborghini Aventador 3,597,431 mentions
2) Audi R8 3,388,955
3) Lamborghini Huracan 2,789,616
4) Ferrari 458 1,684,744
5) Lamborghini Gallardo 1,375,998
6) McLaren P1 1,159,653
7) Honda NSX 1,152,686
8) Ferrari LaFerrari 1,141,428
9) Bugatti Veyron 884,538
10) Bugatti Chiron 806,034
11) Ferrari 488 768,408
12) Lamborghini Murcielago 538,808
13) McLaren 720S 534,462
14) Ford GT 528,610
15) Pagani Huayra 507,802
16) Aston Martin Vantage 479,275
17) Lamborghini Veneno 466,152
18) Ferrari F430 453,965
19) McLaren 570S 391,482
20) McLaren 650S 325,013

136

In a different but connected test to the previous one, a journalist for the Sun newspaper in the UK experimented with two identical Tinder profiles.

In one he used a photo of himself standing next to a Lamborghini Aventador and in the other he used a profile without any car shown at all. Over the following week the profile with the car received 36 matches, the one without got only 16.

136 - 144

And a recent survey by online number plate brokers click4reg.co.uk studied the effect of various types of car on Tinder responses.

The same man got this number of matches from women with these cars in the background:

1) BMW i8 132
2) Audi R8 129
3) Mercedes C Class 98
4) Land Rover 95
5) Nissan NV 69
6) Mini 69
7) No car at all 67
8) Fiat 500 41 (worse than no car at all)

144 & 145

Italian motorsport pioneer Carlo Abarth gave his parents a hint of the future when aged 11 he covered the wooden wheels of his scooter with 'tyres' made of leather belts... so he could go faster than all the neighbouring children.

* Years later, in 1965 at the age of 57, Abarth lost 66lbs (30kg) in weight (by eating a special diet of apples and steak) to squeeze into the tight cockpit of a single-seater Abarth-tuned Fiat racing car to set two world speed records.

146

Upmarket car brand Lexus employed a tattoo artist... to create a promotional version of its UX crossover by 'tattooing' it all over using a tiny hand-held drill. Five days of engraving created a pattern that was then painted red and black with gold leaf details. The transformation cost around £120,000 ($147,000) – although the base car is only worth around £30,000 ($37,000).

147

The development of Britain's motorway system has introduced words such as pile-ups, contraflows, fast-lane and hard shoulder into everyday English language.

148

The Simca brand had a strange, sudden demise at the hands of US parent company Chrysler. In 1976 Simca was flying high as the Simca 1307 was voted European Car of the Year. And in 1978 the Simca Horizon won the same prestigious title. In just two years' time, in 1980, the familiar European Simca badge was scrapped by distant bosses at Chrysler...and no Simcas have been built since.

149

The award-winning Ariel Atom was at one point in 2008 the fastest accelerating production car in the world. The Atom 500 could do 0-62mph in less than 2.3 seconds. Yet the design of the world-famous car was based on a drawing by a transport student at Coventry University.

Niki Smart's undergraduate project was spotted by a college lecturer with links to the automotive industry. Former student Smart went on to become a highly-rated freelance vehicle designer based in Los Angeles.

150

American TV comedian Tracy Morgan picked up his new Bugatti from a New York dealer in June 2019. A short way down the road however he was involved in a collision with an SUV driven by an elderly lady at a set of traffic lights. The comedian leapt from his new car and was seen shouting: "It's a $2 million car. I just bought it!"

151

A survey by leading UK motoring organisation, the AA, found a decline in long-term car ownership. A rise in car finance packages means owners are encouraged to change cars more often. A fifth of UK cars are funded by lease or hire deals. Only a third of all drivers said they planned to keep their current car for more than five years.

152

The youngest ever driver to start a Formula One race was Dutch teenager Max Verstappen, who was aged just 17 in the Australian Grand Prix of 2015...

153

...And the oldest ever driver was Louis Chiron from Monaco, who entered his hometown Grand Prix in 1958, a few weeks short of his 59th birthday.

154 - 158

Four things about Alfa Romeo

1) The pride of many red-blooded Italian patriotic motoring fans is Alfa Romeo. It was founded in 1910 however not by an Italian... but by a Frenchman, Alexandre Darracq.
2) Things went quickly after that though: within 15 years of launching Alfa Romeo won the inaugural world Grand Prix championship in 1925.
3) Enzo Ferrari founded his Scuderia Ferrari motor racing team in 1929 not driving Ferraris (which didn't exist yet) but Alfa Romeos.
4) Alfa Romeo may be a small name in contemporary racing... but it still has the most race wins of any motoring brand in history.

159

Successful Formula One team McLaren set itself an ambitious target when it announced in 1989 it was building the McLaren F1. It was going to be 'the fastest car in the world'. Just 100 were built, each using a BMW Motorsport 6.1-litre V12 engine.

When tested, the F1 accelerated from 0-60mph in 3.2 seconds and reached a sensational top speed of 231mph/372kph. McLaren had achieved its objective: for a decade after its launch in 1992 the F1 was the world's fastest production car.

Chapter six
From building a Cadillac...
To drink-driving plumbers

160

Cadillac won the prestigious Dewar Trophy in 1908 for demonstrating the precision and consistency of its car manufacturing in an extraordinary way:

- o Three standard Cadillac Model Ks were taken from its London showroom, driven for ten laps round the Brooklands circuit, then disassembled completely.

- o The parts were jumbled up and split into three piles. Two mechanics, armed with just wrenches and screwdrivers, then re-built three Cadillacs.

- o These were then roadtested for 500 miles each – and performed flawlessly.

161 & 162

The utilitarian Saab 92 was the Swedish company's first car in 1949. It was considered very aerodynamic but involved a simple construction technique: the entire car was stamped out of one sheet of metal, then the holes for doors and windows were cut out.
All the early models were painted dark green – because Sweden had a surplus of the paint from its wartime aircraft production.

163 - 173
Ten signs you love your car TOO much
(From Holtsauto.com)

1) You worry when parking it somewhere unfamiliar
2) There is a strict list of rules for passengers
3) Some of your most memorable moments have happened in your car
4) Your car has a 'pet' name
5) Your car has a gender
6) Over-expenditure on car air-fresheners
7) Time spent researching your car's model's history
8) Thinking about your car when you're away from it
9) Brief glimpses of random colours, smells or music remind you of your car
10) You find yourself peering out of the curtains at night… just to check it's okay

174

A Canadian study from 1994 found that people who drive with their headlights on during daylight hours are 11 times less likely to be in an accident.

175

When Honda created its luxury Acura brand in 1986 it was the first Japanese manufacturer to try that tactic. Toyota followed with Lexus and Nissan with Infiniti. Acura was a big hit in the USA but was never sold in the UK and strangest of all… has never been available in Japan.

176

An un-named Swedish driver was caught speeding behind the wheel of a Mercedes-Benz SLR in Switzerland at 186mph. Because of the extreme speed and the driver's wealth a huge fine was imposed: 650,000 Euros.

That's around £570,000 or $750,000... and is currently the world-record speeding fine of all time.

177

Lego staff spent much of 2018 building a full-size Bugatti Chiron that can accommodate two, and move and stop. It took the professional team 13,500 hours and more than a million Technic bricks to create the supercar. The Lego Chiron had 2,304 Lego battery-powered motors to propel it... and it could reach distinctly un-Chiron-like speeds (up to 18mph/29kph).

178

One of the worst ever road accidents in the US occurred in Chicago in May 1950 when an electric tram collided with a fuel tanker truck, creating a massive terrible fireball which killed 33 people.

179

The Bentley Bentayga wasn't the luxury brand's first SUV. In 1994 Bentley built six bespoke large four-wheel-drive vehicles for the Sultan of Brunei. The odd special edition Bentleys looked slightly like period Range Rovers with added grand Royal bonnets and front grilles. The 'Bentley Dominators' cost the Sultan a cool £3 million ($375,000,000)... each.

180

Scottish driver Andy Cowan won the 1977 London to Sydney Marathon in a Mercedes 280E. At the time it was the longest rally ever staged. The 19,000-mile/30,000km race took 34 days.

181 - 191

Top ten occupations rated the highest risk for UK car insurance premiums:

1) Professional footballer
2) Any other sportsperson
3) Fast food delivery driver
4) Scrap dealer
5) Apprentice
6) Car wash attendant
7) Student
8) Town clerk
9) Doorman
10) Carpenter's assistant

* The jobs with the lowest motor insurance rankings are: exam supervisors, retirees and curtain-makers.

192

A used 1994 Aston Martin Volante sold for £240,000 in December 2019 because it had been used by Prince Charles for 15 years. The two-door racing green convertible was fitted with a police radio, second 'security' rear-view mirror and leather-trimmed container in the centre console... where Charles kept sugar cubes to feed polo ponies.

193

One of the world's most famous architects designed a petrol filling station in a small town in Minnesota, USA. Frank Lloyd Wright, voted 'the greatest American architect of all time', designed the strangely angular gas station, which opened in 1958. It had a bizarre observation tower ... so the pump attendants could watch for approaching customers.

193 - 203

A survey of UK drivers by online private number plate agents click4reg.co.uk found the most popular phrases uttered during moments of road rage. (The interviewers appeared to remove all swear words.)

1) Go on then move! (72%)
2) Is the person in front dead? (70%)
3) He's not even looking (67%)
4) Of course, it's a BMW (64%)
5) Wow, someone is in a hurry (61%)
6) You're welcome (58%)
7) Learn to use your indicators (44%)
8) You could park a bus there (41%)
9) Who teaches these people to drive? (36%)
10) Are they actually blind? (28%)

204

A study by MoneySuperMarket revealed plumbers have the highest percentage of drink-driving convictions of any occupations in the UK.

Chapter seven
From Renault's Christmas trick…
To a 110-mile traffic jam

205

On Christmas Eve 1898 an inventive 20-year-old engineer
Louis Renault was staying with friends in Paris. He bet them
that his homemade vehicle, a simple four-wheeler with a one-
cylinder engine that he'd made in his father's garden shed,
could climb the steep Rue Lepic, a well-known historic street
in Montmartre.

The car triumphed, Louis won the bet and the feat helped sell
12 cars that night. The achievement kick-started the launch of
the Renault company.

206

State authorities in Queensland, Australia have permitted the
addition of certain emojis on vehicle number plates. Motorists
are able to choose to add the "laugh out loud", "wink",
"sunglasses", "heart eyes" or "smile" emojis to their plate.

207

A little-known piece of motoring safety experts' advice: Try not to grip the steering wheel as you would a tennis racket, with your thumbs wrapped around so they connect with your fingers. Instead, leave your thumbs on top of the wheel. In a sudden collision or over a severe bump, the steering wheel can be whipped back round... and that can break or dislocate your thumbs.

208

BMW purchased the Rover Group in 1994, (the 80% stake cost £800 million) but sold most of it just six years later for a token fee of £10 to a consortium of businesses.

- BMW kept the Mini branch itself and later sold the Land-Rover division to Ford for £1.85 billion.

209

The highest number of sales of one particular car model in one year was achieved by Toyota global sales staff when they managed to shift 1.36 million Corollas in 2005.

210

Whistling Billy was a steam-powered racing car that dominated American dirt track circuits before the First World War. The car was built by the White Sewing Machine Company in 1905. It broke many track records and was often described as 'the fastest car in the world'.

The steam engine ran at around four times the pressure of a steam locomotive and reached such huge temperatures, engine parts often glowed red-hot. It made a distinctive howling sound as it raced down the straights - reaching top speeds around 120mph/193kph - hence the popular name among crowds that came to see it.

In 1912 the car suffered an undignified end however: it crashed over an embankment during practice runs in Portland, Oregon. After turning over, it broke in half.

Sadly the famous steam engine was eventually removed... and fitted into the hull of a steam boat.

211

Nissan uses the number 23 on its motor sport cars because the number 2 translates to 'ni' in Japanese and the number 3 translates to 'san'. So 23 is pronounced 'ni-san'.

212

Experts estimate that between 10% and 70% of people in urban traffic are simply looking for somewhere to park.

213 and 214

Bentley preserved one model of its supercharged 'Bentley Blower' car from 1930 in its heritage collection in Crewe, England. The luxury subsidiary of VW recently decided to use this single remaining example to 'clone' another 12.

The vintage 4.5-litre, 138mph (222kph) sports car is being stripped down to every tiny bolt and nut for 3D scanning. A combination of surviving pre-war original moulds, jigs and hand tools plus 21st-century technology will be used by expert motor engineers at the company's Mulliner division to build a dozen new Blowers.

The project is underway as this book was being written. The cars will be sold to wealthy collectors for 'an unspecified price'.

- **Before Aston Martin's DB5, the Bentley Blower was the first car used by the fictional character James Bond. Secret agent 007 drove a 1931 model in his first appearance (in Ian Fleming's 1953 novel Casino Royale).**

215

In 1900 the young auto engineer Ferdinand Porsche built a prototype car with an electric motor on each wheel, creating an emission-free four-wheel-drive car more than a century before there was a market for them.

The first Porsche-badged sports car appeared on sale almost half a century later, in 1948 – with a petrol engine.

216

Recently VW launched a conversion kit that changes a classic VW Beetle into a fully electric car. The new car uses the drive components from a VW e-Up. Its range is about 120 miles and top speed is 93mph.

The conversion can only be done by VW partner eClassics... and costs a hefty 100,000 Euros (£87,000/$110,000).

217

In 2018 a German 18-year-old was banned from driving after being caught speeding at almost double the limit... just 49 minutes after passing his driving test.

218

The M96 is a fake section of three-lane motorway hidden among farmland in England's rural Cotswolds, complete with correct signage, gantries and road markings.

The 400-yard/370m stretch is used to train fire-fighters to deal with crashes and sometimes serves as a film or advertisement location. It is not open to the public.

219

In the inaugural Indy 500 race of 1911, all but one of the 40 entrants carried a driver plus a passenger, whose job was to warn the driver of the position of other cars behind.

In the 40th car was the youngest son of a Pennsylvania carpenter Ray Harroun, who took the outrageously risky decision to drive alone. Harroun decided to race without the normal observer... but with an eight-by-three-inch mirror on a stand fixed to his dashboard instead. It is believed to be the first use of a rear-view mirror. Being one person lighter and more aerodynamic, Harroun's 75mph/121kph Marmon Wasp easily won the race.

220

Japanese digital game designer Kazunori Yamauchi, who created the Gran Tourismo series, helped Nissan fine-tune the dashboard display of the R35 GT-R. He was given a GT-R in return.

221

As a publicity stunt in 1927, an elderly white-haired Henry Ford drove the 15 millionth Model T Ford out of his Detroit factory with his son Edsel alongside.

- *The Ford plant at Dagenham in East London celebrated its 10 millionth car and Ford's 250 millionth worldwide, when a Fiesta was driven off the production line in 1996 by retired boxing champion (and local resident) Frank Bruno.*

222

The world's longest traffic jam was 110 miles (177km) long. It was in France, between Paris and Lyon in 1980.

223

In 1998, William Allen, aged 84, spent two days on London's orbital motorway, the M25, trying to find the right turn-off for his daughter's house.

Chapter eight

From crashes at junctions…
To the bridge-with-no-name

224

In the USA 40% of car crashes occur at intersections, according to the National Highway Traffic Safety Administration, as do 22% of all fatal crashes.

225

Why is the name Veyron used for the Bugatti supercar?
It derives from the brave story of Pierre Veyron, a test driver for the marque in the 1930s. In the Second World War Veyron became a hero of the French Resistance. He was awarded the highest national honour, the Croix de Guerre in 1945, and then returned to his test-driving and racing career.

226 - 246

A survey by What Car? of UK motorists found that the best car dealers are not necessarily the most prestigious brands. Here are the franchise dealers ranked for customer satisfaction:

The best

1) Lexus
2) Subaru
3) Honda
4) Suzuki
5) Toyota
6) Volvo
7) Skoda
8) Kia
9) Peugeot
10) Hyundai

And the worst...

1) Land Rover
2) Audi
3) Mercedes
4) Renault
5) Porsche
6) Nissan
7) Mitsubishi
8) Vauxhall
9) BMW
10) Mazda

247

Some safety experts claim that one in five UK motorway accidents are caused by drivers falling asleep at the wheel.

* Along stretches of the M1 motorway in England there are normally 'tiredness can kill' warning signs. For the funeral procession of Princess Diana in 1997, these were discretely removed.

248

The Howmet TX was a 1968 single-seat sports car powered by a military helicopter turbine engine. It won two races under the guidance of American owner and driver Ray Heppenstall (no relation).

249

The 1963 Buick Riviera, a powerful sports coupe often regarded as one of history's most beautiful cars, was believed to be inspired by the vague ghostly outline of a Rolls-Royce that Buick design boss Bill Mitchell had glimpsed through a fog in London.

250

Gangster Al Capone owned a fully-armoured 1928 Cadillac to protect him against machine gun attack by rival gangs. The car was impounded by the US treasury department when Capone was sent to Alcatraz prison.

On the evening of December 7 1941, after the shock of the Pearl Harbor attack, the Secret Service needed to transport President Franklin D. Roosevelt in bulletproof security to deliver his "Day of Infamy" speech to Congress.

Someone had the idea to get Capone's car out of storage and use it. When asked where he got such a mysterious vehicle at short notice, the President famously revealed its owner by saying: "I hope Mr Capone doesn't mind."

251

Rolls Royce offered buyers of the Cullinan SUV a miniature version of their car as an extraordinary and expensive optional extra. Customers who ordered the £264,000 ($309,000) luxury SUV could also order a £30,000 ($38,000) 1:8 scale replica.

Rolls claimed the smaller model version contained more than 1,000 parts and took 450 hours to build. Its miniature details even included Rolls' standard branded umbrellas hidden in the door panels and headlights operated by remote control.

252

Up-market motor holidays provider, Ultimate Driving Tours, offers luxury tours in a fleet of supercars. You can choose whether to drive in the Ferrari, Rolls, Bentley or Lamborghini each day. Accommodation is in five-star hotels with gourmet food. The 'Beautiful cars and Michelin Stars' tour offers three days driving and two days eating and drinking, and costs around $16,000 (£13,000) per person.

253

In the UK more than 150,000 motorists put the wrong fuel in their car every year.

254

A car hire company in Essex, England uses a Toyota Previa people-carrier as its promotional vehicle. The Previa is converted into a large green road-legal version of Thunderbird II... and is capable of 90mph (145kph).

255

The 2018 Porsche 911 GT3 RS saved weight in every way possible... including removing the bonnet and boot Porsche badges and replacing them with simple stickers.

- **Aston Martin retorted by fitting the Valkyrie supercar with a weight-saving chemically-etched aluminium badge that's 70 micros thick (ie: 30% thinner than human hair).**

256

In the UK and US a light commercial vehicle with an enclosed cab and open cargo area with low sides and a tailgate is known as a 'pickup' or 'pickup truck'. In Australia and New Zealand however, it is called a 'utility vehicle' or commonly a 'ute'.

- **In South Africa it is called a 'bakkie', a derivation of an Afrikaan word for container.**

257

The impressive Studebaker story started when Peter Studebaker, Master of the German Cutlery Guild, emigrated to the New World in 1736. He built a house and wagon factory near a huge oil shale deposit in Maryland. At the time oil shale was crucial in manufacturing high quality steel.

The family business grew to become the biggest maker of horse drawn wagons in the world, including supplying US Army wagons and transport for the California Gold Rush. Studebakers also built US Presidential carriages.

From 1902 the family expanded into horseless carriages, first with electric-power, then with petrol engines. Studebaker cars quickly became even more successful than its carriages. By 1918 its car production had soared to 100,000 a year, overtaking its horse-drawn carriage business (75,000 a year).

258

…The Studebaker family business boomed after receiving enormous orders cabled urgently from the British government at the start of the First World War. They included 20,000 harnesses for horse-drawn artillery, 60,000 saddles and 3,000 transport wagons.

259 & 260

The Tay Road Bridge in eastern Scotland is the longest road bridge in the UK – and one of Europe's longest. It opened in 1966 and is 1.4 miles (2.3km) long.

- *In 2002 local radio station Tay FM held a vote for a new name for the bridge. The slogan that was clearly winning referred to the gradient on the bridge and the reputation of the city it leads to. "It's All Downhill to Dundee" was rejected as a suitable name however and the poll was abandoned.*

Chapter nine

From a Japanese London cab…
To super-hot brakes

261

One of the commonest versions of the classic London black-cab taxi was launched briefly on the Japanese market. Nissan gave the car what it thought was a suitable British sounding name: The Big Ben.

262 – 267

Tips for survival if your car gets stuck in the snow

- o Put on all the clothes you have available
- o Use car heater for about 10 minutes every hour to keep above freezing but preserve fuel
- o Clear snow from hood, roof and boot to make car visible from air
- o Pile snow around sides as insulation
- o Move around inside car regularly to stay warm
- o Use paper, CDs and dry branches to build a fire in centre of spare tyre to create column of black smoke.

268

The Kia Sorrento Ski Gondola was a 2016 special version of the Korean SUV that dispensed with wheels altogether. Instead it was fitted with four triangular caterpillar tracks to propel the normal five-door family SUV across deep snow.

269

An early UK motorway safety advert from the 1950s warned drivers of the dangers of stopping to enjoy a family picnic in the slow lane of the M1.

270

A Rolls Royce electric concept car of 2016, called the 103EX, featured a bonnet mascot than began to glow as you approached your destination. On arrival a small step deployed by your door and a red illuminated 'carpet' was projected on to the pavement. The concept hasn't made it to full production, yet.

271

Cadillac founder Henry Leland was previously an apprentice at gun-maker Colt and introduced the precision engineering necessary to build revolvers into the automotive world.

272

The Rover 2000 was a pioneering new type of executive car when it launched in 1963, halfway between big old-fashioned luxury limousines and popular family cars.

It featured a unique innovation: a pointed plastic extension on top of the front light lenses. This illuminated extension poked just above the bonnet line so the driver could see the corners of the car in low light and also confirm that the lights were on. It won safety awards in the UK but was banned in some markets as being a danger to pedestrians and so the idea disappeared forever.

273

In 2020 a young Chinese driver who had just passed his test a few minutes earlier accidentally drove onto a pier and plunged into an icy river. The driver, from Guizhou province, managed to escape with a dislocated shoulder. His car was later recovered by crane. The new motorist claimed he was distracted by texts from his friends congratulating him for passing his test.

274

A former fuel garage in Washington, USA is now listed on the USA's National Register of Historic Places. The gas station was built in 1922… in the shape of a giant teapot.

275

Contrary to popular belief the world's first motorway wasn't a German autobahn. It was the Autostrada Dei Laghi, opened on September 21, 1921 – in Italy.

276

The Bugatti 'Voiture Noire' or 'black car' was a one-off supercar built by the French company in 2019. It was capable of 0-60mph (0-96kph) in 2.5 seconds and a top speed of 261mph (420kph). So far its buyer has not been revealed. A press report that it was football star Ronaldo, who already owns two Bugattis, was later denied. The price however was no secret: it cost £12 million ($18m)... making it the most expensive new car ever.

277 - 290

The ultimate driving bucket list

Autocar.co.uk writers were asked to choose their top motoring experiences:

1) Drive a car at 200mph
2) Drive on the Isle of Man's derestricted TT roads
3) A west coast US road trip
4) Do a lap of Iceland (828 miles)
5) Drive a Mini around the Atacama Desert in Chile
6) Spend a day with a Caterham on a hill-climb event
7) Borrow the money and buy your dream car
8) Drive from Cairo to Capetown
9) Drive coast-to-coast in USA
10) Spend a weekend off-roading
11) Import an American muscle car
12) Drive a Bugatti Veyron
13) Restore a barn-find to full glory

291

The carbon brakes on a modern Formula One car need to heat up to around 500°C to become fully effective. They are able to operate effectively up to enormous temperatures of around 1200°C.

Chapter ten
From disliked BMW drivers...
To the world's favourite sports car

292

An analysis of Google search trends surveyed over 2,000 drivers to find the most common impressions people have of drivers of each car brand.

They found:
- o 82% said they dislike BMW drivers, making it the most disliked brand
- o 10% said they dislike Toyota drivers, making it the most liked car brand
- o 7% said they wouldn't date a Volkswagen driver
- o 60% said they think of VW owners as bad drivers
- o 50% of respondents said they dislike Audi drivers
- o 64% thought of Volvo drivers as being slow

293

Ford's Cortina was the UK's best selling car of the seventies. It was named after the Italian ski resort of Cortina d'Ampezzo, site of the 1956 Winter Olympics. As a stunt to promote its new car Ford drove new Cortina models down the resort's Olympic bobsleigh course.

294

Lee Redmond of Salt Lake City, Utah, USA held the Guinness World Record for the longest fingernails. Over 30 years they had grown to a curly 30 inches (76cm) long on each finger. She became a minor celebrity after numerous appearances on TV until a car accident in 2009 when she was thrown from her car... and all the nails broke off.

295 - 296

The term "cranky" originally referred to the bad mood drivers would be in after struggling to turn the crank while trying to start their car.

- **Early car pioneer Byron Carter, founder of the Cartercar brand, was killed trying to start a friend's car in 1908. The car backfired, sending the crank handle violently twisting backwards. It hit Carter in the head.**

297

German luxury car tuner Brabus has launched a special 'Mission' version of the Mercedes G-Wagon SUV. The heavily armoured vehicle with a blast-proof safety cell, bulletproof glass and stab-resistant seats cost £645,600 ($793,000).

298

Jacques Villeneuve was just 11 years old when his father Gilles Villeneuve, a popular F1 driver, tragically died after an accident in a practice session for the Belgian Grand Prix in 1982. But the shock didn't deter Jacques from following his father. He became an F1 champion driver himself, and later a media pundit.

299

The UK's biggest breakdown rescue provider, the AA, receives about 10,000 call outs a day.

300

Police pulled over an SUV driving erratically in a small town in Utah, USA. They were shocked to find the driver was a five-year-old boy.

The youngster had taken his family car and said he was heading to California to buy a Lamborghini. They found he had his savings of $3 with him.

301

Aston Martin's fledgling racing credentials were formed after it surprised the motoring world... by taking all three podium places in the 1933 Le Mans 24 Hour race (with its 1.5L two-seater, open-top roadster capable of 85mph/137kph).

302

The 2017 Dodge Viper SRT-10 coupe featured a tailgate 'snake' badge that illuminated red - to function as a central brake light.

303

After car seat manufacturer Recaro gave a sports seat to a stadium in Augsburg, Germany in 1995, as a light-hearted place for the coach to sit, the idea caught on. Other clubs wanted the ultra supportive racing seats that were designed for motorsport vehicles. Now scores of major soccer stadiums use Recaro seats in their dugouts, including Real Madrid, Bayern Munich and Ajax Amsterdam.

304

Drivers of the 1922 Type 59c Cadillac could fill its tyres at the press of a button… thanks to a built-in air-compressor.

305

Five-time Formula One champ Juan Manuel Fangio didn't like rear-wheel drive cars. He said: "Horses should pull the carriage, not push it."

306

The dignified and serious membership of the British Civil Servants' Motoring Association recently voted for the "100 most iconic cars of all time". In reverse order, the slightly odd top ten were:

10 Citroen DS
9 Audi Quattro
8 Ford Fiesta
7 VW Golf
6 Jaguar Mk II (Inspector Morse)
5 Mini Cooper (Italian Job)
4 Mini (modern BMW version)
3 Jaguar E-Type
2 Aston Martin DB5 (Goldfinger)
1 Range Rover

307

Car-mad Hollywood actor Steve McQueen bought an extremely rare road-going D-Type Jaguar racing car called an XKSS. Only 25 of this early two-seater convertible were built but nine destroyed in a factory fire. One of the survivors was bought second-hand by McQueen who had it refinished in British Racing Green… and often called it his favourite car.

308

Driving in a straight line at 60mph (100kph) it would take just under a month to drive to the moon.

309

Eight cars you may not realise sold over a million times
- Alfa Romeo Alfasud (1,017,387)
- BMW X5 (over 1 million)
- Citroen DS (1.45 million)
- FSO Polonez (1,061,807)
- Porsche 911 (over 1 million)
- Renault 4CV (first French car to sell over 1m)
- Smart ForTwo (more than 1.3 million)
- Volvo 140 (1,252,371)

310

Four cars you may not realise sold so few (these are worldwide sales):
- Lamborghini Reventon (20)
- Bugatti Veyron (450)
- Lancia Stratos (495)
- McLaren F1 (106)

311

The world's top-selling sport car series in history is not an MG, Mazda, Corvette or Mustang. Its Nissan's Z-cars series, in five generations from 1969 to present, has notched up over 1.5 million sales so far.

Chapter 11

From a strange family outing…
To an unfortunate indication

312

Police in Blackpool, UK, pulled over a Vauxhall car and found the driver was just 11 years old – and the passengers were adult members of his family. The adults told police they were fed up with the youngster playing Grand Theft Auto so decided to let him drive a real car instead.

313

When Buick introduced its all-new Riviera luxury coupe in 1986 it offered one feature never seen on a production car before… a touchscreen display. The 'Graphic Control Centre' allowed drivers to adjust functions - including the car's cassette deck sound system.

314

The 1964 launch of the first Ford Mustang was synchronised so it was unveiled at the World's Fair in New York and at Ford showrooms all over the US at exactly the same time. The result was that Ford sold 22,000 cars on the spot and more than 400,000 within the first year, vastly surpassing expectations.

315

The Rover V8 engine was an iconic British power plant used in British cars from 1965 to 2004. Over that era it was fitted to many Rover cars like the P5 and SD1, as well as Morgans, TVRs, Triumph TR8, MGB V8, many Land Rovers. The 2004 Land Rover Discovery was the last mass-produced car to feature the engine.

The surprising origin of the Rover unit however, was General Motors in America. Rover liked the 1960 Buick 215 all-aluminium engine so much it bought the rights, the machines to make it and even persuaded expert staff to move from Detroit to England in 1965, where the V8 became a mainstay of the motor industry for another 39 years.

316

After the launch of the Ford Sierra in 1982, one of Europe's largest motoring magazines, the German 'Auto' group tested the three main saloon car rivals of the day: the Sierra, VW Passat and Opel Ascona/Vauxhall Cavalier against each other in a 100 different ways. The new Sierra won.

317

The average car is the most complex consumer item available. It has more than 30,000 unique parts.

318

Australian F1 driver Jack Brabham won the world title in 1959, 1960 and 1966 and was the only champion to win in his own car. The former garage owner was the founder of the Brabham Constructors Team and the car he drove was called a Brabham. So Brabham won for Brabham in a Brabham.

319

A survey found 16% of Americans admit to never washing their car.

320

One of the most influential car designers of the last 50 years, Patrick Le Quement was responsible for the shape of dozens of cars ranging from the Ford Sierra to the Renault Megane. The Frenchman was involved in the way 60 million cars on our roads look before retiring from the motor industry in 2009. He now designs boats.

321

A 60-year-old British con man repeatedly got away without paying for petrol by claiming he'd forgotten his wallet after he filled up. His unpaid fuel bill at various garages totalled £3,690 when he was caught. Rather than ban him from driving the judge instead banned him from visiting any of the 7,111 petrol stations in England and Wales for two years.

322

At the time of writing Volkswagen owns 12 motoring brands in seven different countries: VW Cars, Audi, Seat, Skoda, Bentley, Bugatti, Lamborghini, Porsche, Ducati, VW Commercial Vehicles, Scania and MAN.

323

A third of the world population drives on the left, two-thirds on the right.

324

How to deal with a deer/sheep/cow in the road (From MensHealth.com)

- Don't take radical evasive action to avoid a collision. It is more likely to cause you harm than making contact with the animal will.
- You're facing an animal so there's no way to tell in which direction it will flee.
- If you have time, sound your horn and flash your headlights to try to scare it out of your path.
- If a collision is inevitable, brake but keep the steering wheel straight.
- At the last second, steer away from the animal's midsection to prevent it from crashing through your windscreen and hitting you.

325

In Switzerland it is illegal to slam a car door after 10pm.

326

Moscow police pulled over an enormous black fully functioning replica of the Batmobile with armoured glass and built-in replica guns mounted on the bonnet – because it didn't have a proper licence plate. The driver, apparently not called Bruce Wayne, was charged with contravening traffic laws and the car was towed away.

327

In 2020, Ford's M-Sport WRC Fiesta notched up yet another finish in the points at Monte Carlo, the 250th consecutive WRC rally in which Ford finished in the top ten.

328

Hollow Mountain gas station in Utah, USA, has become a tourist attraction… because it is largely built in a cave.

329

Leopard furs sourced from Somalia in Africa were used to upholster the 1950 Cadillac Debutante.

330

A local Audi dealer in Lake Forest, Illinois, USA, came up with a cheeky piece of marketing by using a prominent billboard in the his town to announce: "Attention Lake Forest. An Audi R8 GT has been sold in your town. Slow traffic keep right."

331

Only around 50% of Russian households own a car, or 38% of the population. In the USA 84% of the population owns a car.

332

Art student Samantha Webster-Connor from Nottinghamshire, England, held a marriage ceremony with her Mini. The BBC reported Sam saying she "is passionate about my car".

The 18-year-old blonde dressed in a white bridal gown and veil for the ceremony while fellow students acted as bridesmaids, best man and vicar. The wedding was held at her college and was filmed as part of her art project into people's relationship with their cars.

Sam said: "I am highlighting the fact that people treat their cars as humans." She added that her maroon original Mini has a male personality... and she calls it 'Stanley'.

333 - 345

History.Com's 12 most famous TV cars of all time

1) GMC Vandura
   (1983-87)
   The A Team's customised van was packed with gadgets and weapons.

2) Pontiac Trans Am
   1982 – 86)
   In Knight Rider, David Hasselhoff's KITT was a modified Pontiac that could talk.

3) Kawasaki Z1
   (1977-83)
   The sporty rides of LA biker cops in TV's Chips. (Note to History.com: nice choice but they are bikes not cars)

4) Mustang Cobra
   (1976-81)
   Charlie's Angel Farrah Fawcett's car featured a wide blue racing stripe across the top.

5) Ford Gran Torino
   (1975 – 79)
   Detective duo Starsky and Hutch used a 'tomato red' Gran Torino muscle car.

6) Ferrari Daytona Spyder
   (1984-90)
   Super smooth detective Crockett drove the black Spyder in Miami Vice as an undercover cop.

7) Mini
   (1990-95)
   Rowan Atkinson's Mr Bean drove a lime green British
   Leyland Mini.

8) Dodge Charger
   (1979-85)
   The orange muscle car called 'General Lee' was a
   central part of The Dukes of Hazzard.

9) Volkswagen T2A
   (2004 – 10)
   A pale blue and white VW minibus starred in the time-
   bending castaway show Lost.

10) Volvo P1800S
    (1962-67)
    British spy hero The Saint, played by Roger Moore,
    drove the shark-finned Volvo coupe.

11) Batmobile
    1966-68
    Adam West's wheels were based on a Lincoln concept
    car.

12) 'Munster Koach' Model T Hearse Hot Rod
    1964 -66
    Driven by Herman Munster in spooky US sitcom.

346 & 347

The world record for changing a car engine is 42 seconds. A team of five marines from Portsmouth, UK, practised for two weeks then completely detached, removed, replaced and refitted the engine for a Ford Escort saloon in less than a minute in 1985.

- **If you fancy having a go at doing it faster on your own car note that the expert tricks include clamping all fuel and fluid pipes first.**

348

In 2015, an Illinois driver had an indicator stalk (turn signal lever) removed from his arm... after it had been stuck there for 51 years following a car accident.

Chapter twelve

From a new name for an old Trooper…
To a queue of 1,100 Jeeps

351

The Isuzu Trooper SUV is one of the most re-badged vehicles in motoring history. The medium-sized off-roader was produced between 1981 and 2002 during which time it also appeared in various global markets as:

- o Caribe 442
- o Acura SLX
- o Chevrolet Trooper
- o Subaru Bighorn
- o SsangYong Korando
- o Honda Horizon
- o Opel Monterey
- o Holden Jackaroo
- o Holden Monterey
- o HSV Jackaroo

352

The original time machine in the Back to the Future movie was supposed to be a refrigerator. Director Robert Zemeckis became worried that children would try imitating the film and trap themselves inside fridges. So he changed it from a fridge to a 1981 DeLorean DMC-12.

353

Rural roads have a fatality rate 2.5 times higher than city roads.

354

In 1998 Bill Drummond, once of electro pop band KLF, and two friends, drove round the M25 for 25 hours "to find out where it leads".

355

Around 53,000 British internet users ask Google every year what BMW stands for. (It's Bayerische Motoren Werke).

356

Americans risk being accused of 'jaywalking' by crossing a street. The concept, however, was invented by the auto industry in the 1920s to shift the blame of car accidents from cars to pedestrians. At the time, "jay" was a slur synonymous with "redneck" or "hillbilly."

357

The latest DVLA figures show that 56,288 cars were stolen in the UK in the year before lockdown. That works out at one every nine minutes. Just two in every five were eventually returned to the owner.

358

The Cadillac Eldorado Brougham of 1957 aimed to celebrate 'the American lifestyle'… hence a list of luxury features that included a make-up kit for the ladies and magnetic whisky tumblers for the gentlemen.

359

Dutch financier Michel Perridon's Bugatti Veyron was the first in his country. So when his 20-year-old son took it for a joyride - and did 100mph through Rotterdam - it was quite easy for authorities to track down the speeding car and deal with its owner. He was later reported to be 'rather angry' with his offspring.

360

A recent study by road safety experts at IAM Roadsmart in the UK revealed that the latest in-car infotainment systems cause so much distraction to drivers they impair drivers' reaction times even more than illegal levels of alcohol or cannabis.

361 - 366

Five simple mistakes that might invalidate your UK car insurance

- **Forgetting to inform insurers of a change of job**
- **Not passing on any change of address**
- **Ignoring vehicle modifications, these can even include changing the upholstery**
- **Giving a lift and accepting petrol money**
- **Not renewing your license at the age of 70**

367

Eccentric and controversial pop star Brian Harvey suffered serious injuries in 2005 after one of the most unusual car accidents in history. The former East-17 singer felt unwell at the wheel of his Mercedes after eating too many baked potatoes. He opened his car door but accidentally pressed the accelerator instead of the brake and was thrown from the car, which then ran him over.

368

An unlucky Lamborghini owner from Australia had his car seized by police and he had no idea why. The £200,000 Gallardo was impounded on the spot by police, who claimed it had been caught doing 99mph in a 43mph zone. Later the owner discovered a garage mechanic had borrowed it for a joyride. The owner eventually got his supercar returned.

369

During World War I BWM built the aero engine for the Red Baron's triplane.

370

University researchers have analysed UK police and traffic statistics plus data from the Office for National Statistics to deduce that male drivers pose a 'significantly higher risk' to other road users than women.

Men in cars and vans cause twice as many deaths and male lorry drivers cause four times as many as female equivalents. The same applies on two wheels, as male bikers caused ten times more fatalities than women bikers.

371 - 380

Nine owners of classic open-top Mercedes SL sports cars

- o Sophia Loren
- o Clark Gable
- o Frank Sinatra
- o Prince Ranier of Monaco
- o Princess Diana
- o Alfred Hitchcock
- o Grace Kelly
- o Shirley Bassey
- o Sir Stirling Moss

381

12 slang words used to describe damaged, poor, misfunctioning or simply old used cars

Banger, bucket, clunker, bomb, jalopy, heap, crate, shed, lemon, rust-bucket, wreck, death-trap

382

Tatra, now a truck manufacturer in northern Czech Republic, produced its first car in 1897 – making it the third oldest vehicle producer in the world with an unbroken history (after Mercedes and Peugeot).

383

Custom car enthusiast Perry Watkins from Buckinghamshire, UK, spent six years building the world's fastest VW campervan. He removed most of the back of the vehicle and fitted a Rolls Royce jet engine. With a flaming exhaust trail, the huge jet engine could propel the VW to a 300mph (482kph) top speed on the Santa Pod drag race strip.

384

From 1963 to 1982 the compact design of all Corvette sports cars meant they came without any trunk or boot for carrying luggage.

385

English aviation test pilot 'Bob' Moore helped to develop the Saab Tunnan jet plane in Sweden. When he returned home he bought a 1955 Saab 92 back with him – the first ever Saab imported into the UK. Moore later became the first managing director Saab GB.

386

World War One fighter ace and Medal of Honour winner Eddie Rickenbacker returned from the front and established his own car company in 1919. He personally test drove prototypes for 100,000 miles himself before the first Rickenbacker was launched at the 1922 New York Auto Show. The car featured Rickenbacker's squadron logo: a stars and stripes top hat inside a ring. The slogan was: 'A Car Worthy of its Name'.

The company introduced four-wheel brakes and around 35,000 models were sold in five years before financial problems brought the company down, with Rickenbacker personally losing $250,000.

Some car lists...

387 - 402
15 famous individually named fictional cars

- KITT (Knight Rider)
- Batmobile
- General Lee (Dukes of Hazzard)
- Herbie
- Christine (Stephen King novel)
- Bumblebee (Transformers)
- The Mystery Machine (Scooby Doo)
- Shaguar (Austin Powers)
- Mutt Cutts (Dumb & Dumber)
- Chitty Chitty Bang Bang
- Lightning McQueen (Cars)
- Bluesmobile (Blues Brothers)
- Brum (UK kids TV show)
- FAB1 (Thunderbirds)
- Genevieve (Fifties film)

403 - 415

12 pairs of very different cars with the same engine

- o Mercedes A-Class & Dacia Duster both used the 1.5-litre Renault diesel engine
- o BMW 320i & Citroen DS4 used a PSA EP6 1.6-litre petrol engine
- o Smart ForTwo & Nissan Micra shared the same Mercedes 3-cylinder petrol engine
- o Maybach GLS & Aston Martin Vantage used the same Mercedes petrol V8
- o Ford Mondeo V6 & Noble M400 used the same Ford 3.0-litre Duratec engine
- o Toyota Camry V6 was fitted with the same Toyota 2GR-FE engine as the Lotus Evora
- o Volvo XC90 and the Noble M600 used the same Yamaha V8 engine
- o Audi S6 and Lamborghini Gallardo LP560 used the same VAG V10 petrol engine
- o Citroen C5 & Range Rover Sport shared the same Ford 3.0-litre diesel unit
- o Mini One and Toyota Corolla were fitted the same Toyota 1ND-TV diesel unit
- o Ford Fiesta & London Taxis shared the Ford Endura 1.8-litre diesel engine
- o Ford Galaxy people carrier and Volvo C70 convertible used the same PSA 2.0-litre diesel engine

416

The world's big car brands are occasionally based in famous cities but more often in towns you may not have heard of.

Aston Martin, Gaydon, Warwickshire, UK
Audi, Ingolstadt, Germany
Bentley, Crewe, UK
BMW, Munich, Germany
Bugatti, Molsheim, Alsace, France
Buick, Detroit, Michigan, USA
Cadillac, Detroit, Michigan, USA
Caterham, Crawley, West Sussex, UK
Changan, Chongqing, China
Chevrolet, Detroit, Michigan, USA
Chrysler, Auburn Hills, Michigan, USA
Citroen, Paris, France
Corvette, Birmingham, Alabama, USA
Dacia, Mioveni, Romania
Daihatsu, Osaka, Japan
Dodge, Auburn Hills, Michigan, USA
Ferrari, Maranello, Italy
Fiat, Turin, Italy
Ford, Dearborn, Michigan, USA
Great Wall, Baoding, China
Hindustan, Kolkata, India
Honda, Tokyo, Japan
Hyundai, Seoul, South Korea
Isuzu, Tokyo, Japan
Jaguar, Coventry, UK
Jeep, Toledo, Ohio, USA
Kia, Seoul, Japan
Koenigsegg, Angelholm, Sweden

Lada, Tolyatti, Russia
Lamborghini, Sant'Agata Bolognese, Italy
Lincoln, Dearborn, Michigan, USA
Land Rover, Coventry, UK
Lotus, Norwich, UK
Mahindra, Mumbai, India
Maruti Suzuki, New Delhi, India
Maserati, Modena, Italy
Mazda, Hiroshima, Japan
McLaren, Woking, Surrey, UK
Mercedes: Stuttgart, Germany
Mitsubishi, Chiyoda, Tokyo, Japan
Peugeot, Paris, France
Nissan, Yokohama, Japan
Opel, Russelsheim, Germany
Peruda, Serendah, Malaysia
Porsche, Stuttgart, Germany
Proton, Subang Jaya, Malaysia
Renault, Boulougne-Billancourt, Paris, France
Rolls Royce, Goodwood, West Sussex, UK
Seat, Martorell, Catalonia, Spain
Skoda, Mlada Boleslav, Czech Republic
Smart, Boblingen, Germany
Ssangyong, Pyeongtaek, South Korea
Subaru, Ebisu, Tokyo, Japan
Suzuki, Hamamatsu, Shizouka, Japan
Tata Motors, Mumbai, India
Tesla, Palo Alto, California, USA
Toyota, Aichi, Nagoya, Japan
Vauxhall, Luton, UK
VW, Wolfsburg, Germany
Volvo, Gothenburg, Sweden

417

In 1979 safety officials in the US insisted that new cars' speedometers went no higher than 85mph... whatever the true top speed of the vehicle. Within three years however the authorities had revoked that rule because they found it hadn't had any effect on real road safety.

418

British singer George Michael crashed his Land Rover into a Snappy Snaps photo kiosk during a Gay Pride parade in London in 2010 and was charged with driving while unfit through drink or drugs.

419

The Rockne was a 1930s American car brand named after a college football coach. Acclaimed Notre Dame University coach Knute Rockne died in a plane crash in 1931, triggering a national outpouring of grief. He was honoured on a postage stamp, roads were named after him and more than 100,000 mourners attended his funeral.

The Studebaker automobile company, based near Notre Dame University, promptly launched the Rockne marque with two models: the "65' and '75', and later the '10'.

By 1933 the project was abandoned as a flop, mainly due to the economic depression. Leftover parts were sent to Norway, Rockne's homeland, where they were assembled and sold as complete cars.

420

The Renault Espace F1 was a special version of the boxy French people-carrier produced to celebrate the company's motorsport heritage in 1995. The brick-like MPV featured an Espace body, painted black and gold, with the chassis and running gear of a Renault-Williams Formula One car. It had four seats, 800bhp... and could do 0-120mph in 6.9 seconds.

421

At the end of World War Two, American troops on the Pacific Island of Espirito Santo were told to dump their vehicles because it was too expensive to transport them all back to the USA. The troops built a slipway into the sea and spent days driving jeeps and trucks down it, jamming the accelerators and leaping out at the last moment. 'Million Dollar Point' on the remote island has now become a popular location for divers to visit the massive underwater scrapyard.

422

Six cars owned by Prince William and Kate Middleton (according to buzzdrives.com)

- Range Rover
- Jaguar XJ
- Bentley Flying Spur (armoured)
- VW Golf Mk IV (Kate's original car)
- Aston Martin DB6 Volante (their wedding car)
- Audi R8 (William is such a fan he invited Audi bosses to his wedding and this is the only non-British car in Royal family collection)

423

The 1953 Ferrari 375M racing car was considered so beautiful and desirable that rich buyers pestered the company to make a road-going version. Enzo Ferrari decided to make just five 'Speciale' road models but he would have to approve each buyer personally.

Film director Roberto Rossellini wined and dined Enzo and persuaded him to sell him an 'Ingrid grey' Speciale as 'a gift of love' to his film star wife Ingrid Bergman. Unfortunately when Roberto unveiled the car for his wife she didn't like its muscular race-bred styling and, to Roberto's horror, she never drove it.

*Rossellini promptly sold the car he'd struggled so hard to buy and what was now globally known as the 'Bergman Coupe' eventually became part of the collection of Microsoft executive Jon Shirley.

424

In 2011 a three-mile-long slow moving parade in Butler, Pennsylvania, USA, set a new world record – it was composed entirely of 1,106 Jeeps.

Chapter Thirteen

From the Welsh valleys…
To the official Jeep face-mask

425

Gilbern Sports Cars was founded in Wales by former butcher
Giles Smith and German glass-fibre expert Bernard Friese. The
company name was a combination of the first parts of both
business partners' names. It made cars between 1959 and 1973
in the unlikely location of a small village called Llantwit Fardre
in the Rhondda Valley.

426

**The logo for BMW is a distinctive black circle with
interior quarters in alternate blue and white. Despite car
enthusiasts calling it the BMW propeller, the colours were
designed like this merely to represent the regional colours
of Bavaria where the headquarters of BMW is located.**

427

*They may now make futuristic supercars in Sweden but the Koenigsegg
family is able trace its roots back to a chivalrous knight of the Holy
Roman Empire who was based in Bavaria, Germany, in 1171.*

428

The prestigious European Car of the Year award is actually run by magazine journalists. The award was established in 1964 and is now organised by these car magazines

Auto (Italy)

Autocar (UK)

Autopista (Spain)

Autovisie (Netherlands)

L'Automobile (France)

Stern (Germany)

Vi Bilagare (Sweden)

429

The five areas of the UK where drivers have the most penalty points on their driving licences:
- **Halifax, Yorkshire**
- **Bradford, Yorkshire**
- **Huddersfield, Yorkshire**
- **East London**
- **Wakefield, Yorkshire**

430

One of the most important cars produced in the last 100 years in engineering terms is hardly known out of Italy. The Lancia Lambda was launched in 1922 and was the first car to feature a load-bearing unitary body and to use independent suspension. The Lambda also used a pioneering shock absorber system and unusually for the time had a four-wheel braking system. Even the engine was unusual: it was the first production car with a V4 configuration.

431

Club branded merchandise offered for sale by the Morris Minor Owners Club UK

- o   Black leather gear lever knob £11
- o   Woollen beanie hat £8.50
- o   Bodywarmer £25
- o   Black flat cap £12.50
- o   Club tie £7.50
- o   40th Anniversary club tie £6
- o   Toiletry bag £8
- o   Drinks coasters (set of four) £9
- o   Cushion cover £16.50 (£30 for two)
- o   Gift wrapping paper £1.50
- o   Morris Minor Christmas Cards (set of ten) £6.50
- o   Wall clock £10
- o   Tea towel (pair) £6

432

American website ConsumerReports.com polled 168,000 customers who were dissatisfied with a car workshop repair. The reasons for their grumbles were:

- o   38% Price too high
- o   28% Did not properly fix problem
- o   21% Took longer than expected
- o   18% Repair didn't work
- o   11% Price more than estimate
- o   8% Car not clean when collected
- o   7% Sold unnecessary parts or service
- o   6% Treated poorly by staff
- o   4% Had to wait more than 30mins after being told car was ready for collection
- o   3% Staff tried to take advantage of my gender

433

Moustachioed British auto-pioneer and colourful businessman Frederick Simms first introduced the words "petrol" and "motorcar". He also designed the first armoured car, founded the Royal Automobile Club (1897) and the Society of Motor Manufacturers and Traders (1902), and strangely, in 1907, discovered a previously unknown waterfall in the Austrian Alps, now called Simmswasserfall.

434

The 1954 Mercedes 300SL is often considered to have been the world's first supercar. It was the first production road car with direct fuel injection and could hit 154mph. A standard road-going production model competed against the leading specialist racing cars of the era in the 1955 Mille Miglia. It came a creditable fifth.

435

The seven cars that make the best hot rod conversions, according to JMC Automotive of Delaware, USA (Hot rodding involves modifying a classic car with a bigger engine and visual enhancements)

- VW Beetle (Mark I)
- Ford Model T (1929)
- Lincoln Zephyr (1937)
- Mercury Hardtop (1950)
- Willys Coupe (1933)
- Ford Roadster (1932)
- Ford Coupe (1933)

436

Three facts about speeding

1) Drivers with a conviction for speeding are twice as likely to crash as those with none

2) On a clear road, the range for a mobile speed camera can be as high as two miles

3) The limit starts at the point you pass the speed limit sign... and ends as you pass the de-restriction sign

437

Iraq dictator Saddam Hussein's Uday son collected gold-plated pistols and cars. It is believed he owned more than 1,000 cars. Most disappeared during the Iraq War but coalition forces discovered these cars in his garages after the end of hostilities:

o *Ferrari F40*
o *Ferrari 550 Maranello*
o *2 x Porsche 911*
o *Porsche 928*
o *BMW Z1*
o *Various Rolls Royces*
o *5 x Excalibur Phaeton (specialist American retro roadster)*
o *Plymouth Prowler*

438

In the seventies BMW was well ahead of the market by developing a pioneering electric car. It built its first electric vehicle in 1972 called the BMW 1602e. Sadly, this never made it to the market because it could only reach half the speed of its other models... and could hold a charge for only 20 minutes.

439

Former Prussian blacksmith August Horch got a job working in Karl Benz's pioneering motor workshop in Germany, in 1896, just 11 years after Benz had patented the first-ever car. Within four years however Horch had learned enough to leave and set up his own car making operation. He called it Audi.

440

Just before the global pandemic the little-known Japanese-conceived Aspark Owl became the world's fastest accelerating production car.

The outrageous £2.6/$3.2million supercar was powered by four electric motors to a 249mph (400kph) top speed. It accelerated from 0-62mph in 1.69 seconds and from 0 to 186mph (300kph) in 10.6 seconds.

The Aspark was a carbon two-seater with gull-wing doors and a host of electronic driving aids. Motors produced a record-breaking 1,985bhp of power, twice the output of a Formula 1 car but with a driving range of 280 miles.

The sleek ground-hugging design made it one of the world's lowest riding vehicles with ground clearance adjustable between 80 and 160mm (3.1 and 6.3 inches). The whole car is less than a meter tall. Only 50 were due to be built in Turin, Italy.

441

In 1995 Car & Driver magazine in the US tested the Volvo 850 T-5R estate car and found it 'the quickest wagon in America'. The block-like stationwagon was available in black or bright yellow, wore a sporty bodykit and the 2.3-litre five-cylinder engine was tuned to produce 240bhp. The result was an estate car that could carry a wardrobe but also sprinted from 0-60mph in 6.7 seconds with a 149mph (240kph) top speed.

442

Five tips from 'mindfulness experts' about what to do when pulled over by the police in the UK:
(The UK hasn't reached the position that American motorists face, where they are advised to keep their hands in plain sight to avoid being shot)

1) Pull over when it is safe to do so
2) Stay inside your car, roll down the window and turn on the inside light
3) Be polite
4) Be mindful of impostors and don't be scared to play it safe
5) Afterwards, take a moment to calm down before continuing on your way

443

Traffic stops are the second most dangerous situation that a police officer has to deal with on a regular basis, so he/she will be on their guard.
(Domestic incidents are the most dangerous, in case you were wondering)

444

The headquarters of BMW in Munich, Germany, was designed to represent the shape of a four-cylinder engine.

445

Second-generation Mercedes SL sports cars, introduced in 1963, are known as Pagodas because of the shape of the hardtop roof and the side pillars holding it up. Somehow it looked like far eastern architecture and the nickname stuck, although there was no official recognition of the Pagoda name. (Just as there was never, officially, a Ferrari Daytona).

446

The largest number of motor vehicles in any country in the world is in China, where there are 340 million. 250 million of these are cars.

447 - 454

Seven items of official branded Jeep merchandise

Jeep fitted hipster men's trunks

Jeep leather dog collar

Jeep levitating speaker

Jeep barbecue set

Jeep barbecue apron

Jeep stroller/push-chair

Jeep cotton face-mask

Chapter Fourteen

From the world's longest lasting model…
To the roads where it's quicker to cycle

455

The name 'Chevrolet Suburban' was first used in 1934 on an early station wagon. After 13 generations Chevy were still selling Suburban people-carriers as this book went to press – making it the world's longest ever production model.

456

Sports car specialists Porsche built a one-off five-door estate in 1987. It was based on the 928 Coupe and company bosses were so unsure about the idea that the car was kept hidden from the public until 2012.

457

Alfa Romeo's twin-cam engine was a long-running powerplant fitted to sporty cars from 1954 until 1994. It was an advanced all-alloy engine with complex double overhead camshafts. In Italy it was revered as an iconic performance unit with a distinctive inspiring sound. Among locals the engine still has an endearing nickname: the 'bialbero' – 'the twin shaft'.

458

In 1927 Frank Lockhart set a record for the fastest lap of a track of wooden boards popular in America at the time. His record average of 147.2mph on the Atlantic City track in a Miller 91 rear-drive single-seater lasted until 1960.

459

Experts advise that before driving onto a sandy beach or the desert, let air out of your tyres. Reduce the pressure to much less than half its normal amount. This helps prevent the car sinking into the sand.

- *If you do start to sink, keep your momentum going. Do not stop. If you really are getting stuck, reverse and look for a another firmer way forward.*

460

The Bugatti Veyron and Chiron supercars each have ten radiators - to keep their monstrously powerful engines cool.

461

During a pit stop in the Tripoli Grand Prix in 1933 British racing driver Henry Birkin bent over to pick up his cigarette lighter and burnt his arm on a hot exhaust pipe. The wound turned septic and Birkin died a month later in hospital.

462

Lamborghini and BMW agreed to jointly build a high performance car in the 1970s. It was designed by Italian Giugiaro and BMW provided much of the suspension and engine. Everything else was provided by Lamborghini. But the Italians suddenly pulled out of the project for financial reasons leaving BMW to hire Baur, a private coachbuilder, to take over Lamborghini's part in the project. The project was far from a disaster and led to the birth of the original BMW M1 supercar.

463 - 467

Latest figures from the American National Insurance Crime Bureau show that on average 85 vehicles are stolen every hour in the US. That's 748,841 a year.

- o   In Mid-West states Ford or Chevy pick-ups are the most frequently stolen.
- o   On the West Coast, Honda Civics are most at risk and in the east Honda Accords, Chevrolet Impalas and Toyota Tacomas are most vulnerable.
- o   And for some unexplained reason the lone state of Wisconsin had a different pattern, with the Dodge Caravan (a people carrier) being the most stolen vehicle.

468

The New York to Paris road race in 1908 was one of the longest, craziest marathon events ever organised. Only six cars took place but a huge crowd of 250,000 gathered in NYC to cheer them off. The 22,000-mile/35,000km race took six months and some contenders started with no driving licence and learnt to drive as they went along.

The winners – by one of the biggest margins in any race in history - were Americans Montague Roberts and George Schuster in an open-top Thomas Flyer 50/60 who beat the German Protos team by 26 days.

469

Volvo's first bid to build a sports car resulted in the pretty fibreglass P1900 roadster, launched with fanfare in 1956. It soon transpired however that the car was underpowered and badly built. Sales were a disaster and Volvo cancelled production after just 67 models were made.

470

Test drivers at Bonneville Salt Flats in Utah, USA, wear sun cream on the inside of their noses because of sunlight reflecting upwards from the shiny white salt.

471

The Ferat Vampire was a special one-off Skoda 110 Super Sport made for a Czechoslovak horror film in 1982. In the film, the car ran on human blood. In reality, the black-and-red mid-engined coupe ran on petrol of course. It was carefully preserved and is still displayed at Skoda headquarters at Mlada Boleslav.

472

Early McLaren cars featured a prominent black Kiwi bird logo. The national bird of New Zealand was chosen to represent owner Bruce McLaren's homeland. The kiwi was later dropped for a series of racing chevrons and eventually the more modern single stylised chevron that now appears.

473 - 482

Nine car companies that also have made tractors

- Aston Martin
  For 25 years the British sports car maker was owned by tractor-maker David Brown, hence the DB series of sports cars.

- Lamborghini
  Ferruccio Lamborghini founded his 'Trattori' company first, then his supercar brand. The tractor business was sold in the seventies.

- Ford
  The Model F tractor of 1917 was a pioneering lightweight, mass-produced, petrol-powered farm vehicle. Ford made successful tractors until 2000.

- GM
  General Motors' Samson tractor brand tried to match Ford, failed, and lost the company around $33million in the process.

- Porsche
  Between 1956 and 1963 Porsche built 125,000 tractors that were popular across Europe. They were, of course, sleek and nimble.

- Fiat
  With a tractor division since 1919, Fiat is one of the world's biggest manufacturers of farm vehicles. Its tractor empire includes New Holland, Ford Tractors and Case.

- Mitsubishi
  Mainly focussing on the compact class of tractor, Mitsubishi targets smaller sized Asian farms. It does sell in the US however, under the Cub Cadet brand.

- Honda
  The world's largest motorcycle manufacturer also makes everything from lawnmowers to supercars. It has built more 100 million engines, which have powered tractors, ATV and various farm machines.

- Renault
  After the First World War when French manufacturer Renault built armoured tanks, it turned to farm vehicles using the same engine and tracks. They were tested on owner Louis Renault's farm in Normandy. By 1938 Renault was the largest builder of tractors in France but eventually sold its tractor division in 2008.

483

Mercedes almost took over its deadly German rival BMW during a difficult period for the Bavarian manufacturer's finances. BMW had almost gone bankrupt by 1959 and Daimler-Benz, Mercedes' parent company, attempted a hostile takeover. BMW fought back, enlisting its shareholders and even humble factory mechanics to buy shares to thwart the takeover bid.

484

In the 1991 Canadian Grand Prix Nigel Mansell was clearly in the lead on the last lap and slowed to wave to the crowd. The Williams-Renault car's electronic management was confused by the unpredictable manoeuvre and, sensing a problem, disengaged the clutch. Mansell coasted helplessly as Nelson Piquet caught up, overtook and took the chequered flag.

485

Until 1988 Australian cars were built with no legal rules governing the accuracy of speedometers. They could perfectly legally display wildly inaccurate speeds.

486

The odds of dying in a car accident during your life are generally given as around 1 in 5,000. By comparison the odds of dying in a plane crash are 1 in 11 million.

487 - 488

The brand name Mercedes came from an Austrian who sold and raced German Daimler cars in the South of France at the turn of the 20th century. Emil Jellinek named his racing cars 'Mercedes' after his daughter. The name stuck a chord and was then given to a series of official Daimler cars. The label, which is originally Spanish for 'mercy', stuck and has become one of the best known brands in the world.

- **Mercedes Jellinek didn't share her father's love of cars, however, and died tragically in Vienna... in post-war poverty.**

489

A 55-year-old truck driver from Pennsylvania, USA, was driving on the Route 422 in 2011 when he choked on a lump of the apple he was eating. He couldn't breathe and passed out... but as the out-of-control articulated lorry ploughed into a concrete barrier the impact dislodged the apple and saved his life.

490 - 491

When Hans Werner Aufrecht and Erhard Melcher formed a Mercedes tuning company in Grossaspach in 1967 and launched AMG (based on the three initials), they decided on making a statement with their first creation.

It was an outrageous version of a sedate 300 SEL saloon. AMG kept the wood panelling and carpeted floors but added bigger wheels in bigger arches, a roll-cage and a fire-breathing, highly-tuned 6.8-litre V8 producing 428bhp. The car was soon universally nicknamed 'The Red Pig'.

* In its first outing the first AMG defied the expectations for a large, gas-guzzling saloon. The Red Pig surprised everyone by coming second at Spa 24-Hour Race.

492 - 496
Four everyday things almost as bad as drink driving
(From the Royal Automobile Club)

o Driving while dehydrated
You may top up your car's fluids but driving in a hot car can cause significant loss of water to a point where your concentration and o-ordination are significantly affected. Mildly dehydrated drivers that were studied at Loughborough University made twice as many errors like drifting out of lane or braking too late.

o Hayfever pills
Around one in five suffer from pollen reactions and most take medication at some point. Antihistamines can cause drowsiness, blurred vision and increase reaction times.

o Jetlag
Driving home from the airport after a long haul flight can be dangerous. Disturbed sleep patterns make you less able to concentrate and prone to sudden feelings of sleepiness.

o Herbal tea
Limited studies suggest that some herbal teas, like chamomile, lavender and valerian, have a sedative affect. Adding honey as a sweetener to any drink may also inhibit alertness.

497

Engineer Colin Fallows, a 50-year-old grandfather and trained mid-wife, broke the British land speed record in 2000... driving a homemade car. The 'Vampire' became the first vehicle to record 300mph (482kph) on British soil after Colin fitted the engine from an old RAF jet engine that he bought for £500 ($628).

498

One of the most important parts of BMW corporate branding for more than 65 years has been a distinctive double curved opening at the front of the car called 'a kidney grille' (first seen on the 303 model of 1933).

499

Researchers estimate that in the Japan's congested capital Tokyo, a bicycle is faster than a car for most journeys of under 50 minutes.

Chapter 15

From Kylie Minogue…
To the truth about speed cameras

500

The BBC reported that a painting of Kylie Minogue wearing gold hotpants hanging in the window of an art gallery in the British seaside city of Brighton in 2003 was causing severe traffic hold-ups - because drivers were slowing down so much to take a better look.

501

Since 1914 Chevrolet vehicles have worn a badge usually called 'the bow-tie'. It still features today but has evolved into a graphic 3-D cross symbol.

There are two theories about where the original bow-tie logo came from:

- Chevy founder William Durant saw it on French hotel wallpaper, liked it so much he tore a piece off and took it back to America.
- It was a copy of the 'Coalettes Coal' logo Durant spotted in a Virginia newspaper ad promoting 'the little coals with the big heat'.

502

The first UK speed limit was introduced in 1861, with the Locomotive Act. The limit was set at just 10mph. However legislators soon felt that even this was too fast and the 1865 Act reduced it significantly. New road speed limits were 4mph in the countryside and 2mph in town – and in addition drivers had to send a pedestrian ahead with a red flag or lantern to warn others of their approach.

503

In 2020 Volvo announced it would install a limiter on all its new vehicles, restricting the top speed to 112mph (180kph). And extra device will be included, allowing owners to limit the car's speed still further if required (down to 30mph/48kph if required).

504

Porsche may be one of the great names of sports cars but it has only ever won one Formula One Grand Prix. This was in the 1962 season after American driver Dan Gurney had failed to finish in the first three races.

At the fourth, the French Grand Prix, he was an unfancied contender in the middle of the field when all the cars in front started suffering technical problems.

One-by-one they withdrew. Gurney found himself alone in the lead and was able to drive his Porsche to the company's only ever F1 victory.

505

A standard Saab 9-3 four-door, two-litre, automatic saloon reached an impressive selling price of 465,000SEK (around £37,500 or $46,500) at auction… because it was the last Saab to be built.

The car had been the last of a final run of 9-3s produced in 2014 by NEVS who had taken over the bankrupt brand. It was intended for further testing and had 40 miles/70km on the odometer, purely from driving around the factory area.

The pristine 'diamond silver' car had stood unsold and forgotten at the factory in Trollhattan, Sweden for five years. It was bought by an un-named Saab enthusiast.

506

Tip to start a dead battery

(from Menshealth.com)

If your battery terminals are corroded, crack open a can of cola and pour it directly onto the battery terminals. The acid in the cola will bubble away the corrosion, improving both your connection and the odds of a successful jump-start. Once you're home, run water over the battery to remove the cola residue and dry it with an old rag.

507

It is an offence to drive a vehicle in reverse on any part of a UK motorway.

508

In a recent survey What Car magazine found the UK's slowest depreciating new car was the Alpine A110 mid-engined sports car. The A110 cost £47,810 new but retains 65.4% of its value over three years.

The most depreciating, in contrast, was the Peugeot 308. The 1.5 HDi version of this family hatchback depreciated so quickly that after three years it was worth just 21.9% of its original price tag.

509

An extraordinary one-off Spanish sports coupe called the Pegaso Cupula was displayed at the 1953 New York Auto Show. The bright yellow two-seater had red-wall tyres, a large glass rear canopy and a chromed side-exhaust under the passenger door. The unique design appealed to the President of the Dominican Republic who was visiting the show and he bought it on the spot. The car stayed in the Caribbean for 30 years before ending up in the Louwman Museum in The Hague, Netherlands.

510

Largely forgotten today, Borgward was a successful German car manufacturer between 1890-1963. It produced the premium Isabella range in the fifties but closed in the midst of controversial financial dealings in 1961.

Its name is preserved by enthusiasts like the UK Bogward owners club based in Birmingham, which has "more than 100 members" and a Borgward Owners Club in the USA, based in Long Island, which doesn't publicise membership numbers. In addition, Borgward Isabella T-shirts are available globally via online mail order in 16 colours.

511 - 514

Are you sitting comfortably? Three trivial things about sitting in a car:

o   The Daily Mail reported that sitting for a long time in a car with the heated seat turned on could be a threat to male fertility. It reported a scientific study that found the electric-generated heat in a man's lower regions could affect his reproductive organs.

o   An average American driver spends 67 minutes each day behind the wheel. Men who keep a wallet in their back pocket raise one hip above the other, twisting their spine and straining the lower back. It can put pressure on your sciatic nerve, a common source of lower-back pain.

o   Men's Health magazine advises: If your car doesn't have adjustable lumbar supports, simply roll up a towel and place it behind you to fill in the small curve between your waist and hips. The more you support your spine, the less your back will ache.

515

When BMW's M10 four-cylinder engine first hit the streets in 1962, the unit produced just 75 horsepower. By 1983 the company's engineers had spent decades fine-tuning the same basic engine design... until it could achieve 1,400 horsepower in Nelson Piquet's Brabham, which he drove to the Formula One World Championship. Cynical observers claimed he won the title with 'a 20-year-old street-car engine'.

516 - 517

Edgar Hooley, surveyor for Nottinghamshire County Council in the UK's Midlands, was out for a walk in 1901 when he made a world-changing discovery.

He noticed a stretch of a country lane was unusually smooth and asked locals why. They told him a barrel of tar had fallen off a cart and people had poured on stones and waste from a nearby iron works to try and clear up the mess. Hooley realised the result was a vast improvement on normal muddy, rutted surfaces.

While Scotsman John McAdam is often credited with the invention of tarmac, Hooley perfected it by making the stones stick to the surface. He patented the accidental mix of tar, stone and iron slag and oversaw the world's first tarmac road surface: a five-mile stretch of Radcliffe Road in Nottingham.

- *Wealthy local MP Sir Alfred Hickman saw the potential, bought the idea and in 1905 formed the Tarmac company that is still in operation today.*

518

A Valentine's Day survey by an insurance company found that almost one in five drivers claim to love their car as much as their partners. One in 20 admitted they preferred their car.

- Over a third (36%) considered their car as either male or female (roughly the same for each sex)

- Around 15% of drivers call their car by a name, with 'baby' being a favourite, followed by Josephine, Elise, Freya, Chilli, Mervyn and Beast

- Almost one in three said their vehicle was comparable to their partner because it 'makes me happy', a quarter said that 'it never lets me down', and a fifth said 'it's easier to handle'.

- 19% said 'it's cheaper to run' and 18% 'it doesn't answer me back'

519

The Argyll Turbo GT was an exciting mid-engined sports car produced in Dumfries, Scotland, in 1976. It was a collection of parts from other manufacturers. The sleek fibreglass body was powered by a Renault V6, with the addition of Datsun Cherry lights, Volvo dashboard and Morris Marina door handles.
Top speed was claimed to be 160mph (260kph) and the price £25,000 (roughly the same as a contemporary Ferrari). Twelve were built, but sadly none were sold.

520

The official Transport for London website, where drivers simply pay for the city's car congestion charges, published a list of dozens of scams and 'alternative' ways of paying that all involve paying more than the official charge. Some charged extra administration fees and others just take all your money and leave you with a fixed penalty for non-payment.

521

'The Brass Era' describes the early period of US car manufacturing before World War One. Brass was commonly used as an eye-catching material for headlamps, radiators and brake levers for high-wheeled, horseless carriages of this time.

522

The 1978 South American rally was one of the toughest in an era of popular long-distance races. The 18,000-mile (29,000km) rally covered the entire continent. Mercedes entered an unlikely team of luxurious 450 SLC Coupes with standard engines and amazed watchers by taking first, second and fourth places.

523

A modified black and orange Bugatti Chiron driven by Andy Wallace recorded a sensational top speed of 304.8mph (490kph) during track testing in 2019. Top Gear commented: "That's over three times the top speed of a Suzuki Jimny."

524

The VW Brasilia was a Brazilian-made, standard-looking three-door hatchback that was unfamiliar across the rest of the world. It was made between 1972 and 1984 as a successor to the Beetle and sold a million models. Despite its Polo-like styling, it was more like the Beetle under the skin: with its engine in the rear luggage space between the rear seats and tailgate.

525

Erwin 'Cannonball' Baker set 143 driving speed and endurance records between 1912 and 1941, including driving across America faster than a train, driving a ReVere prototype to 48 state capitals and driving a Franklin sedan/saloon to win an extreme hill-climb event: racing up to the summit of the 6,260ft (1,908m) Mount Washington.

526

The UK Dept of Transport says that for drivers over 25, speeding is a factor in only 2% of injury road accidents.

527

The iconic French car of the inter-war years, the Citroen Traction Avant, was actually also built in large numbers in the suburban town of Slough, England.

Most were made in Paris but 25,000 of them were built in the unlikely setting of a trading estate in the unglamorous Thames Valley town. These right-hand-drive versions for the British market were given smarter wooden dashboards and Smiths instruments. The pioneering front-wheel-drive vehicles were advertised as: "The take-you-anywhere car."

528

In 2020 website uk.motor1.com (perhaps bored during a pandemic lockdown) compiled a list of the current production convertible cars with the fastest roof lowering mechanisms.

The results were:

> 15 seconds: BMW i8 roadster and Lexus LC Convertible
> 14 seconds: Aston Martin DB11 Volante and Ferrari Portofino
> 13 seconds: Mazda MX-5 RF
> 12 seconds: Jaguar F-Type Convertible and Porsche 911 Cabriolet
> 10 seconds: Audi TT Roadster and BMW Z4
> 9 seconds: Porsche 718 Boxster
> 7 seconds: Ford Mustang Convertible
> 6.7 seconds: Aston Martin Vantage Roadster (although it takes 6.8 seconds to raise)

529 - 534

Hidden in the UK statute books are some obscure little-known motoring laws. These five are all offences:

- Driving on UK roads with dirty number plates
- Flashing your lights to warn other drivers they are approaching a speed trap
- Drinking a glass of wine in a parked motorhome
- Sitting in a stationary car with the engine running
- Travelling with your dog unrestrained in the cabin of your vehicle

535

In 1964 British sports car manufacturer AC was spotted testing a racing car at 185mph before the Le Mans 24 Hour race… on the M1 public motorway.

This was before UK motorways were given a speed limit but it still created a storm of controversy in the press. By 1966 the government set a limit of 70mph as a temporary experimental measure to see if it reduced the number of accidents. A year later the limit was made permanent.

AC test driver Jack Sears, who had been using the M1 for his pre Le Mans warm up, said the new limits were nothing to do with his 185mph runs.

536

When electric car pioneer Tesla launched on the market it helped generate sales by including a buy-back guarantee. This meant owners had the reassurance that they could sell their Tesla back to the company after three years for an agreed price. Any that were sold back were refurbished by Tesla and sold as used vehicles at a profit.

537

One of the lowest points in the history of the Aston Martin was in 1924. Playboy Count Louis Zborowski, fabulously wealthy Astor family heir and chief financial backer of Aston Martin was killed after losing control of his car and hitting a tree. Aston Martin went bankrupt shortly after.

538

The Mercedes SL of 1989 was the first car to offer an automatic roll protection hoop that was said to deploy in a third of a second if sensors showed the car was about to turn over. Enthusiastic Mercedes drivers are said to have discovered it would also deploy if driven over a hump-backed bridge at a high enough speed.

539

The famous TT motorcycle circuit on the Isle of Man uses normal public roads as its racetrack. For the rest of the year the country and mountain sections of this course have no speed restrictions at all and are often used by high-speed supercars and superbike enthusiasts despite also carrying normal traffic, buses and cyclists too.

540

AC Cars claim to be Britain's oldest vehicle manufacturer "having been in continuous production since 1901".

541

Police officers in Arizona pulled over a suspicious driver using the less congested 'high-occupancy' lane of a busy route. They found the 62-year-old driver had dressed a skeleton in clothes and a hat, and strapped it into the passenger seat alongside him.

542

Businessman Nicola Romeo took over Milan-based car-maker Alfa in 1918 and combined his name with theirs. He died in 1938 but was so popular that there are still three Via Nicola Romeos commemorating him (two in Milan, one in Naples).

543

Honda engines powered the entire 33-car starting field of the 2010 Indianapolis 500.

544

When he was away from the cameras American car-mad actor James Garner, who played Firebird-driving seventies TV detective Jim Rockford also competed in off-road races. Garner was such an enthusiast he built his own car called 'The Banshee' as a dirt track hot-rod. It was based on a 1972 Oldsmobile Cutlass with a fibreglass body and 480bhp V8 engine. The shortened body meant the enlarged engine sat right in the passenger compartment. Garner said it helped balance the weight distribution and he could reach over to tune the carburettor while driving. Garner drove the 144mph Banshee to victory in an off-road race before turning over on a corner and badly damaging it. The machine was rebuilt and is now owned by a US motoring enthusiast.

545

Arrol-Johnston was a little-known pioneering car manufacturer based in the East End of Glasgow, Scotland, between 1895 and 1931.

It produced the world's first "off-road" vehicle for the Egyptian government, and another designed to travel on ice and snow for Ernest Shackleton's expedition to the South Pole. It also built the first production automobile manufactured in Britain, the six-seater, wood-bodied 'Dogcart', which was started by pulling hard on a rope.

546 - 549

A survey by AutoExpress magazine found that most UK police roadside speeding cameras have a leeway of 10% plus 2mph, so a vehicle has to be travelling at a true speed of 79mph in a 70mph limit to activate the camera.

- o On the other hand, a car speedometer is not allowed to 'under-read' – they can't tell you you're going more slowly than you really are. Most new vehicles produced around the world are allowed to have speedometers that over-read by up to 10 per cent plus around 4mph/6kph. So they could read 81mph at a true 70mph. In USA it's slightly less, with a 10% permitted variation.

- o According to this you could be doing an indicated speed of 90mph on your dashboard and still not trigger a speed camera set for 70mph.

Chapter sixteen

From Sao Tome...
To a Corvette ZR-1

550 - 551

The islands of Sao Tome and Principe together form a country off the west cost of Africa. It has the lowest rate of car ownership in the world, with only two cars on average between every 1,000 residents.

- *In comparison, the world's highest motoring ownership is in the tiny wealthy enclave of San Marino in Italy, which has 1,263 vehicles per thousand people.*

552

The 1963 Mercedes SL is remembered as a glamorous, luxury car... but it was also a safety pioneer. The SL was the first sports car to be fitted with a rigid passenger safety cell and special front and rear crumple zones.

553 - 559

Six six-wheeled cars

- o Tyrell P34 (F1 car) 1976
- o Covini C3A (supercar) 2004
- o Pullman York (luxury car with powered middle axle) 1903
- o Dodge T-Rex (six-wheel-drive off-roader) 1997
- o Panther (8.0-litre convertible) 1967
- o Mercedes G63 AMG 6x6 (military off-roader) (2007)

560

During a life of around 100,000 miles (160,000km) the cooling belt in a car engine typically endures around 100 million revolutions.

561

In the US passenger car bumpers must be able to absorb a 5mph (8kph) impact from another vehicle without causing damage to the car body.

562

The AVE Mizar of 1973 was a brave prototype that featured a combination of Ford Pinto... and a Cessna Skymaster light aircraft. Full production was planned to start in 1974. Californian company Advance Vehicle Engineering had built a prototype version of car, which could be attached and detached from the Cessna wings and powerplant easily and then driven normally on the road. Tragically, when development engineer Henry Smolinski and Harold Blake, AVE Vice-President, took the Mizar for its second test flight, the wing buckled in mid-air and the Ford plunged to earth - killing both occupants and ending the project forever.

563

In the early sixties racing driver Johann Abt was given his own car by team bosses at Abarth. He was told he could race the car for free – if he won all the races he entered. It was a challenging target but Abt almost succeeded: he won 29 out of 30, coming second in the 30th. Abt later founded German motorsport specialists Abt Sportsline, while Abarth eventually became part of Fiat-Chrysler.

564

The Beardmore Super Sports of 1923 was built in Glasgow, Scotland, and priced at £750. Each car came with a certificate that guaranteed that it had been driven around Brooklands racing circuit at 70mph (110kph).

565

The Sun newspaper reported that UK drivers spent an average of 115 hours stuck in traffic over the previous year. Not surprisingly London was the worst spot for jams and was rated the eighth worst city in the world for traffic hold-ups.

566

A learner driver taking her driving test in Bellevue, Washington State, USA, drove back to her driving school with her examiner at the end of the test in October 2015. When she got there she tried to park outside the driving school but accidentally stepped on the accelerator instead of the brake. She careered, with the examiner, straight through the school's window leaving the car inside the building… and failing her test.

567

The 2020 coronavirus lockdown in the UK prompted PSA dealers – that's Peugeot, Citroen and Vauxhall – to offer owners an "anti-bacterial refresh" service for their cars. It included cleaning the air-conditioning, replacing pollen filters and full disinfection. It cost £99 ($120).

568 - 573

Five tips for getting a repair performed right
(from Consumer Reports.com)

- o Describe the problem fully. Give the garage/workshop as much information as possible. Write down the symptoms and when they occur. If possible, talk directly to the mechanic who will be working on your car.

- o Don't offer a diagnosis. Avoid saying what you think is causing the problem. You may be charged for any repairs the shop makes at your suggestion, even if they don't solve the problem.

- o Request a test drive. If the problem occurs only when the car is moving, ask the mechanic to accompany you on a test drive.

- o Ask for an estimate. And have them contact you for approval if the repair will cost more than the estimate.

- o Ask for evidence. If you're not comfortable with the diagnosis, ask the shop to show you the problem parts. Worn brake pads or rusted exhaust pipes are easy to see. Don't let the mechanic refuse your request by saying that his insurance company doesn't allow customers into the work area.

574

Tragedy struck on 23-year-old Riccardo Paletti's first start in F1 racing at the Canadian Grand Prix of 1982. Didier Peroni in pole position stalled on the starting grid and Paletti's car crashed into the back of the stationary Ferrari, caught fire and he was killed.

575

A recent study by pollution monitoring scientists found micro particles caused by the wear to car tyres may be doing more damage to people's health than the emissions from the exhaust pipe.

576

Car trips usually take 10 to 15 percent longer than planned, says Leon James, professor of psychology at the University of Hawaii and the author of Road Rage and Aggressive Driving.

577

- ❖ The Wraith Black Badge is currently the fastest car in the Rolls Royce line-up.
- ❖ At the time of writing it costs £288,410/$355,713 and weighs more than three tons and has a limited top speed of 155mph/250kph.
- ❖ The huge luxury saloon can accelerate from 0-62mph/100kph in just 4.5 seconds.

578 - 579

For 13 years from its first edition in 1978, the soap opera Dallas was one of the most popular television series in the US and Britain. A total of 357 episodes about Texan oil and cattle barons were filmed and made the fictional Ewings one of the world's most famous families.

Part of the characterisation of stars Pam and Bobby Ewing was their bright red Mercedes SLs. Villainous JR meanwhile drove more sinister S-Class models. His first was a dark green 280 SE, then a silver-green 450 SEL.

The red SLs of Pam and Bobby were most iconic though and today, more than 40 years after the show, enthusiasts still turn up at the Dallas location, South Fork ranch in Texas. Mercedes SL owners love to take photos and selfies of themselves and their cars outside the Ewings' home.

- The SL was THE screen car of the era, also appearing prominently in Hart to Hart, Starsky & Hutch, the A-Team and Miami Vice. In films it was a partner to Eddie Murphy in Beverly Hills Cop, Richard Gere in American Gigolo and Sharon Stone in Casino.

580

Experts claim loud or up-tempo music slows your reaction time. The Royal Automobile Club Foundation named Wagner's "Ride of the Valkyries" the most dangerous piece of music to play while driving.

581

When a racing driver turns into a corner early, taking a defensive line, to block an overtaking car from overtaking on the normal racing line, it is called 'shutting the door'.

582 – 591

Nine things about Paddy Naismith

- o Born in 1912, she became an acclaimed film actress in her teens
- o From 1929 she took up motor racing
- o She raced in a green leather jacket to contrast with her bright red hair
- o Paddy drove a car with built-in cocktail bar, fold-down bed and scent spray system
- o In 1930's 761-mile John-O'Groats-to-Brighton rally she was the only driver to do all 40 hours continuous driving alone
- o She won races at the original Brooklands Circuit in an MG Lagonda
- o In 1932 RAC Rally, she drove the entire continuous 1,000-mile course single-handed
- o She was employed to drive Prime Minister Ramsay McDonald on official engagements
- o Paddy became a successful pilot, then Britain's first air hostess in 1935 and volunteered to serve as a flying ambulance pilot in the war
- o Baird's first colour TV test transmission in 1940 was a photo of Paddy Naismith

592 - 603

The 11 quickest cars of the eighties

(From caranddriver.com)
0-60mph times

11 Ferrari Testarossa – 5.0secs

10 Ferrari 288GTO – 5.0secs

9 Ferrari 512BB – 5.0secs

8 Porsche 911 Turbo Cabrio – 4.9secs

7 Buick Regal Grand National – 4.9secs

6 Lotus Esprit Turbo SE – 4.8secs

5 Porsche 911 Carrera 4 – 4.8secs

4 Buick GNX – 4.7secs

3 Pontiac Firebird Trans Am (turbo V6) – 4.6secs

2 Porsche 911 Turbo – 4.6secs

1 Chevrolet Corvette ZR-1 – 4.5secs

Chapter seventeen

From sleeping in the car…
To cheating at Formula E

604

UK drinkers who decide to sleep off a drinking session in the back of their car instead of driving it can still be fined. "Being in charge of a vehicle while above the legal limit" can result in a fine of £2,500 and a driving ban.

605

The risk of having an accident increases fivefold if you are carrying two or more teenage passengers.

606 - 614

Eight strange sounds coming from your car – and what they could mean:

- A low hum - Could be a worn wheel bearing
- Droning noise - Could be worn tyres or suspension
- High squeal - Could be accessory drive belt slipping
- Whine while turning steering wheel – Could be a faulty steering pump
- Low clunks – Could be suspension or exhaust fittings
- Grinding sound – Could be worn brakes
- Extra engine rumble – Could be leaking exhaust
- Unbalanced wobbling on smooth roads – Could be a wheel or tyre problem

615

In 2020 the average age of a Rolls Royce buyer was 43.

616 - 617

The 1970 London to Mexico Rally was sponsored by British newspaper the Daily Mirror and created great excitement at the time. Many unusual cars were entered alongside serious professional rally teams.

British rally champion Bill Bengry entered in his friend's Rolls Royce Silver Shadow. The luxury limousine was adapted with 60-gallon fuel tanks, over-the-roof exhausts and stiffened racing suspension. There were eight additional foglights and a bull bar on the front. The eccentric team tied a tiny blindfold on the Flying Lady bonnet mascot. Sadly the Rolls still wasn't suited to the gravel sections and was forced to retire early. Other early retirements included a Ford Cortina, Fiat 2300 Estate, Austin Maxi, Jeep Wagoneer and VW Beach Buggy.

- **The 16,000-mile (25,700km) race was won by Finn Hannu Mikkola's works Ford Escort, powered by an 1850cc engine. Finishing an impressive sixth, also in an Escort… was the unlikely figure of English football star Jimmy Greaves.**

618

For ten years from 1965 the Buick Gran Sport was GM's premium brand muscle car offering an opulent level of trim and equipment. Consequently they were advertised as 'gentleman's hot rods'.

The 7.5-litre V8 engine of the GSX version of 1970 produced a huge amount of pulling power, or 'torque'. Its 510 lb-ft (691 Nm) power set a new record for torque output of any American production car, a record which lasted until 2003 and the arrival of the Dodge Viper SRT-10.

619

For every actual crash, drivers experience 11 near crashes, according to a study by the Virginia Tech Transportation Institute in the USA.

620

Piero Dusio was a professional footballer for Italian team Juventus... and a winning motor racer. In 1923, after seven years with the soccer club, he retired through injury. Dusio became a successful businessman (selling uniforms to the Italian army) and bought sports cars. He took up race driving in his late thirties and promptly won the Mille Miglia, Stelvio Hillclimb and finished sixth in the Italian Grand Prix.

621

In February 2019 an unthinkable alliance was formed: life-long rivals BMW and Mercedes joined forces to launch an elaborate app-based global car-sharing scheme. They planned to invest a billion Euros to launch their 'ShareNow' scheme in 90 cities that year, then "expand tenfold".

By December however the co-operation between the German premium car rivals appeared to have come unstuck. The scheme was abandoned in the US, Canada, UK and in fact everywhere but for a handful of German cities.

622

Swedish supercar maker Koenigsegg is based in Angelholm on the far west coast of the country... in a former headquarters of the Swedish Airforce.

623

The Brooklands Circuit in Surrey, England, was the world's first purpose-built motor racing venue in June 1907. During World War Two it was closed and used for aircraft production - but never re-opened for racing.

624

Star Bayern Munich footballer Kingsley Coman wound up in trouble with his club in 2020... by driving the wrong type of car. The club had a sponsorship deal with German car-maker Audi but Coman turned up to training in a McLaren 570S. Coman blamed a broken wing mirror on the Audi he had been supplied with, while club officials threatened to fine him £50,000.

625 - 626

In 1919 Ernie Holmes had struggled for hours to pull his Model T Ford from Chickamauga Creek just outside Chattanooga, Tennessee, USA, using bricks, wooden beams and ropes. Eventually the enterprising DIY engineer devised a vehicle with a winch system that could do the job in future. Using a chassis from a 1913 Locomobile, a premium car of the time, he built the 'Holmes 485' in his shed. It was the world's first tow truck and was so good, Ernie patented it.

Holmes tow truck business was soon booming and still exists within the Miller Industries group in Tennessee.

- *Because of this story the state of Tennessee is still the centre of the tow truck world: it also hosts The International Towing and Recovery Hall of Fame and Museum.*

627

The Citroen DS is often chosen as one of the most beautiful and important cars ever built, and boasted pioneering use of important new motoring technologies like disc brakes, pneumatic suspension and distinctive aerodynamic styling.

Surprisingly, the heavy, complex, expensive French luxury four-door family car was also an unlikely rally success. The DS was a strong performer in marathon endurance rallies, won the 1000 Lakes Rally in 1962 and won the Monte Carlo Rally in 1959 and 1966.

628

A Manchester Toyota dealer helped to build the world's biggest-ever sandwich. Castleford Toyota supplied the high-power electric forklift truck used to construct the giant tuna and sweetcorn sandwich to promote the opening of a new supermarket (and enter the Guinness Book of Records). The Toyota sandwich weighed an extraordinary two tonnes.

629

In November 2015, police in Mountain View, California, USA, pulled over a car for moving too slowly. When the traffic cop strolled up to the driver's door, he found there was no one inside to reprimand. There was no driver. The vehicle was a self-driving Google prototype.

630 - 634

According to rentalcars.com, the UK's four most haunted roads are:

- A75 in south-west Scotland
  Sightings on 'The Ghost Road' include horsemen riding across the road in front of cars, eyeless phantoms in the hedgerows and a tweed-wearing elderly figure.

- A229 in southeast England
  A young bride was killed in a crash on her way to her wedding and now haunts the road. Police get regular reports of crashes... but arrive to find nothing there.

- M6 in northwest England
  Phantom sightings include lorries, hitchhikers, Civil War cavaliers and Roman soldiers.

- A616 in northern England
  With high accident rates 'The Killer Road' has been plagued by sightings of ghosts of children lost in nearby mine shafts. Locals have reported hearing a mysterious banging noise... on the roof of their car.

635

The first Ford cars built in 1903 used engines made by Dodge (a part of the rival Chrysler group since 1928).

636

The best-selling car of all-time is PROBABLY the Toyota Corolla, which sold 30 million times in 150 countries around the world. But incomplete global factory records for rivals like the VW Beetle, Ford F-Series and VW Golf make the claim hard to prove.

637 - 638

The shortest Interstate highway in the US is I-95 in South Carolina, which measures just 0.11 miles or 580ft/177m.
And the longest is the I-90 from Newport, Oregon on the west coast to Boston, on the east, which is 3,020 miles (4,860km) long.

639

Two very different motoring pioneer entrepreneurs, American Henry Ford and Frenchman Andre Citroen were firm friends who traveled huge distances to meet many times, discussing and sharing ideas about their respective cars and factory methods.

640

At the start of the 1969 Le Mans 24-hour race Belgian driver Jacky Ickx ignored the traditional starting system, where the drivers sprinted across the track holding their helmets and jumped into the cars to get away.

Instead, he calmly walked across the track, carefully shut his door, slowly fixed his safety belts and set off last in his Ford GT40.

It was a one-man protest against the running start, which he claimed was unsafe. A driver had been injured the previous year when trying to close his door after starting at speed.

Ickx was doubly successful. He ended up winning the race despite his slow start ... and race officials abandoned the old-style running start in the future.

- The tragic proof of his point was that unlike Ickx British racer John Woolfe ran to his car but crashed at the first corner. He was not properly strapped in yet and was killed.

641

According to the Guinness Book of Records the world's longest car was built by Jay Ohrberg of Burbank, California, USA in 1986. The 100ft (35m) white stretch limousine had 26 wheels, a swimming pool and helicopter landing pad.

642

The Citroen factory in Paris made more than 23 million artillery shells during the First World War.

643

One of the most iconic cars in India's recent motoring history, the Maruti 800, was the result of a campaign to create a true home-built people's car by President Indira Gandhi.

In a huge televised ceremony in December 1983, she handed the keys of a brand new Maruti to the humble moustachioed Harpal Singh, an office worker who had won the massive national lottery for the honour of having the first car off the production line.

This particular tiny white 796cc three-door hatchback became famous and the proud Singh attracted crowds wherever he went. He drove it until his death in 2010.

> o *Since then his original prize-winning car has been restored and used as a promotional vehicle by Maruti, which is now India's largest car manufacturer.*

644

In 1998 the new large Volvo saloon, the S80, was chosen as 'the most beautiful car in the world' by judges from the Italian motoring organisation and the magazine Automobilia.

645

The elegant Cord 810 was launched in America in 1936 featuring recent technical innovations like independent front suspension, front-wheel drive and stylish pop-up headlights... which had to be cranked into an upright position using a winding system operated from the dashboard by the driver.

646 – 652

Cheap Lada cars imported from Russia in the eighties gave rise to a wave of jokes about their quality.

Here are six typical ones:

- *Owner asks his mechanic: "Can I get a windscreen-wiper for my Lada?" The mechanic replies: "That sounds like a fair swap."*

- *First prize in the raffle is a Lada. Second prize is two Ladas.*

- *How do you double the value of a Lada? Fill the petrol tank.*

- *What do you call a Lada in the summer? An oven. What do you call a Lada in the winter? A freezer.*

- *How do you avoid speeding tickets? Buy a Lada.*

653

During the global Covid lockdowns Formula-E racing took place online. Drivers used sophisticated simulators instead of real cars.

In the fifth round, Audi driver Daniel Abt suddenly started performing way better than he had previously – prompting an investigation by race authorities. They noticed his face had been obscured throughout the webcam coverage and after the race he didn't join live interviews. Eventually it was found Abt had enlisted a professional expert sim-racer to pilot his machine in his place. Abt was disqualified and ordered to pay €10,000/$11,000/£9,000 fine to charity.

Chapter 18

From competitive roofs…
To a couple arguing over a car

654 - 655

When BMW bought Rolls Royce it spent £65 million ($80m)
building a new factory for the marque on the aristocratic
Goodwood estate near England's south coast in 2003.
Acclaimed eco-architect Nicholas Grimshaw gave the building
Britain's largest living roof: it spreads for eight acres and is
covered with succulent sedum plants.

- *Ford promptly went even better in the same year: it installed
  what it claimed the world's largest living roof on its Dearborn
  truck plant in Michigan, USA. It's also covered in sedum and
  spreads for ten acres.*

656

**Experienced Swedish woman driver Nettan Lindgren was
furious when former F1 driver Jonathon Palmer
deliberately punted her BMW M3 off the track during a
BTCC race at Snetterton in the UK in 1991.**
**Palmer's car ended in the gravel - so Lindgren marched
over to it and was seen shouting and gesticulating at him.
As he tried to get out she slammed the door in his face
and marshals had to intervene and separate them. Palmer
was later disciplined.**

657

The official length of a race circuit is calculated by measuring the inside white line and the outside white line, adding them together and dividing by two.

658

The best four-cylinder car engines of all time

(According to hotcars.com)

15 Honda F20C – a two-litre twin-cam famous for its 8800 rpm redline in the S2000 roadster

14 Mercedes M111 – fine German engineering of the 1990s, especially with 'Kompressor' fitted

13 Mitsubishi 4G63 – turbo power for the 90's Evo

12 Alfa Romeo Twin Spark – two sparkplugs per cylinder added smooth performance from 1986

11 Subaru EJ25 – punchy flat-four from the Impreza

10 Nissan SR20DET – supplied nineties turbo power for the Sylvia & 180SX

9 Toyota 3S-GTE – what made the 2nd-gen MR2 so good

8 Saab B234 – big turbo power for the 9000 Aero

7 Honda B16A – this first VTEC was game-changer

6 Mazda B6ZE (RS) – the simple, reliable reason MX-5 conquered the world

5 Ford EcoBoost 2.3L – 310bhp and 24mpg

4 Toyota 4A-GE – dependable multivalve from '83 to '98

3 Volvo Redblock – robust power for 200 series from 1974, many still going strong

2 VW E-Motor – the air-cooled flat-four behind the Beetle & Campervan from 1936 to 2006.

1 Ford Model T – the pioneering 20bhp four-pot that changed the car world

659

British TV soap star Amy Childs posed seductively on a wrecked car for an insurance commercial... and within a week had to be pulled from the wreckage of her own wrecked car. The glamorous star from The Only Way is Essex wore cropped shorts and gold high heels for a MoneySupermarket advert. She was sitting on the bonnet of a smashed car bearing the personal number plate 'WEII JEL' referring to her catchphrase 'well jealous'.

The actress bought the personalised plate for £80,000 but a few days later her Range Rover Autograph Sport hit a kerb in East London, turned several times in mid-air and came to a rest after demolishing two traffic lights. Amazingly she escaped from the overturned vehicle unscathed. The Range Rover was a write-off but Childs was spotted quickly removing the expensive number plate before it was towed away.

660 - 680

Classic and Sports Car magazine picked the 20 cars that are "undervalued classics from the 70s"

1 Lotus Elan Plus 2

2 Jenson-Healey

3 BMW E3 3.0Si

4 Fiat Dino Coupé

5 AC 3000ME

6 Mazda RX-7

7 Porsche 928

8 VW Scirocco Mk1

9 BMW E21 323i

10 Ferrari 400

11 Triumph Stag

12 Lancia Fulvia Coupé

13 Alfa Romeo Spider S2 Kamm tail

14 Maserati Indy

15 Opel Monza

16 Porsche 924

17 Jaguar XJS

18 Bentley T1

19 Citroen CX

20 Talbot Sunbeam Ti

681

The first known motor race for women drivers was held in Paris in 1897. Eight women competed, all on De Dion motorised tricycles. The winner, Léa Lemoine, was presented with a bracelet.

682

Norwegian sailor's son Jan Wilsgaard was an extraordinarily long-lasting chief designer at Volvo. He was in charge of car design for 40 years, drawing its cars from 1950 until 1990. He became best known for his simple, boxy estate cars and deflected critics by saying "the car is square and sluggish, just like the Swedes themselves."

683

A young driver in a BMW with severely tinted rear windows accidentally reversed into a police car because he couldn't see it, a court in Leicester, UK, was told.

684 - 685

Arizona after-market motoring specialists Eikon offer to fit gull-wing doors to existing motorists' cars. Their spectacular scissor-door kits can fit various vehicles, including those from Acura, Dodge and Chevrolet. Price? Around $3,000 (£2,400).

- *Meanwhile Canadian workshop Webb Motorworks are offering a replacement electric motor for your gas-guzzling engine – while keeping the look of your old engine. The British Columbian company offers a high-performance electric motor built inside what appears to be a small-block Chevy V8.*

686

The DAF Daffodil was a small two-door saloon built in the Netherlands in the sixties. The 65mph (105kph) budget car featured an innovative continuously variable transmission, a new type of automatic gearbox. Its slogan was 'The new fast daffodil – fully automatic' – which inspired a popular Manchester eighties & nineties Indy pop group called the New Fast Automatic Daffodils.

687

At the 1970 Tokyo Motor Show normally conservative Japanese manufacturer Mazda celebrated its 50th anniversary by unveiling an extraordinary concept car: the RX-500.

This futuristic wedge-shaped, mid-engined supercar had plastic bodywork and two sets of gull-wing doors, one set for the cabin and one set to access the pioneering 982cc rotary engine. This could spin at 15,000rpm – more than double the revs of any car at the time.

The interior was trimmed in green and brown leather and the car was said to be capable of 150mph (240kph).

The back end of the car, shaped vertically like the rear of a van, illuminated green during acceleration and red while braking. Of course the RX-500 never made it to production... and the little-known prototype still sits in a Japanese motor museum.

688

Italian-Canadian accountant Sergio Marchionne became CEO
of two struggling car-makers: Fiat in 2004 and Chrysler in
2009. Marchionne, usually seen in his signature black jumpers,
oversaw the amalgamation of the two very different companies
to create the world's seventh biggest car manufacturer.
By his death in 2018 he had created a booming, successful
global business... and in the process paid off their huge
combined debt of $13bn (£10bn).

689

**Citroen launched its GS Birotor GZ model in October
1973 – unfortunately coinciding exactly with the Middle
East Oil Crisis where fuel prices suddenly rose 400%. The
technologically innovative Birotor was doomed because
its twin rotary engine was very powerful, very smooth...
and very thirsty. One test recorded a consumption of just
9mpg. Sales were so poor (847) that Citroen tried to buy
all the cars back and scrap them.**

690

More stories about Aston Martin

- After the Second World War, Aston Martin owner
  Gordon Sutherland realised his company faced such
  financial problems he placed an advert in The Times
  saying: "High class motor business for sale, £30,000."
- British tractor manufacturer David Brown saw it,
  negotiated the price down to £20,500... and promptly
  took over.

691

Early 20th century auto pioneer, businessman and racing driver Alexandre Darracq at one point produced one-in-ten of all the cars built in France... and personally broke the land speed record.

Then in a complete U-turn he sold his business, gave up car manufacturing... and instead went to quietly run a casino in the French coastal resort of Deauville.

692

In 1965 the Corvette sports car was finally fitted with disc brakes: a safer, stronger and longer lasting alternative to the previous drum brakes. The car's conservative fan-base was resistant to change though and 316 American buyers insisted on having the old-style drum brakes fitted – for which they received a $64.50 reduction in the price of the car.

693

Swede Rickard Rydell trained as an accountant with a firm of florists before a dramatic switch in careers to become a racing driver. He promptly won the 1998 British Touring Car Championship in a Volvo S40.

694

In the UK, one in every hundred people change their car every year.

695

The Bristol Car Company was founded in a disused aeroplane factory in the English city of Bristol after the end of the Second World War. For 70 years it built small numbers of high performance saloons but never advertised, preferring to rely on 'word of mouth'. Customers included Liam Gallagher, Tina Turner and Richard Branson. After financial problems, however, the company disappeared in 2020.

696

In the movie Fast & Furious 4 stunt engineers adapted a normally staid Buick Grand National saloon car to drive very fast in reverse (as part of scene robbing an oil tanker). The solution was to fit the engine in the boot and alter the drive system so the car was actually driving forward although the body was facing backwards.

A small driver sat out-of-shot in the back operating the car normally - while actor Vin Diesel sat in driver's seat pretending to drive and steer at seemingly very high speeds in reverse.

697

In May 2020 thedrive.com reported on an American classic car lover who had immediately separated from his partner and filed charges against her after she sold his beloved '67 Chevrolet Impala restoration project to a scrapyard. The girlfriend said she was trying to clear space in their garage.

Chapter 19

From the world's iciest road...
To one of the most expensive clocks
on the road

698

The iciest road in the world is probably the McMurdo
Highway, which runs for 995 miles (1600km) between
McMurdo Station and Scott Station... in Antarctica. It's the
planet's most southerly road and was created by levelling the
ice with snowploughs and filling in cravasses. The route is
simply smoothed ice, marked by a long series of flags.

699 - 710

The 11 fastest accelerating cars between 2010 & 2020

(From caranddriver.com)

11 Lamborghini Urus – 3.1secs
10 Chevrolet Corvette – 2.8secs
9 Porsche 911 GT3 RS – 2.8secs
8 Tesla Model S P90D – 2.7secs
7 Ferrari 488 Pista – 2.7secs
6 McLaren Senna – 2.7secs
5 McLaren 720S – 2.6secs
4 BMW M5 Competition – 2.6secs
3 Porsche 911 GT2 RS – 2.5secs
2 Lamborghini Huracan Performante – 2.3secs
1 Porsche 918 Spyder – 2.1secs

711

A recent survey of the UK's "most outrageous" car repair bills published in the Sun newspaper found one driver had paid £22,655 ($28,661) to have the engine of their 2012 BMW 5 Series repaired.

712

The only major car factory in the Netherlands is the Nedcar works in Born. The plant is one of the most versatile operations in the world. It has produced cars for a wide variety of owners since it opened in 1967.

These have included vehicles as different as the DAF 33, Volvo 480, Mitsubishi Space Star, Smart ForFour, Volvo S40, Mitsubishi Outlander, Mini Countryman and BMW X1.

713

A Citroen driver smashed into a parked car at full speed...
while trying to catch a spider running around inside his
car. The smash on the A50 in Derbyshire, England, was
reported by local police who added that the driver
escaped with minor injuries but was later reported for
driving without due care and attention.

714

The Queen had the leather back seats and armrest of a luxury
Daimler Double Six removed and replaced by a long dog bed
for her pet corgis.

The limousine was delivered to Buckingham Palace in 1984
and used for six years before being returned to Daimler with
29,000 miles recorded. It was recently sold to a collector at
auction for £80,000 ($100,000).

715

During the global pandemic crisis Jaguar Land Rover
flew car parts into the UK from China in suitcases to try
to keep car production going.

716

How to do heel-and-toe gearchanges

This driving technique was required for pre-sixties non-synchromesh gearboxes. Now it is only used by motorsports drivers to help them go faster round corners.

Robby Gordon, winner of three Baja 1000s, explained how to 'downshift like a racer':

"Use your foot to apply the accelerator and brake at the same time," he said. "As you apply the brake, keep your right foot on the right side of the pedal so you can rock your foot over and use your heel to blip the throttle, which raises the revs and allows the car to drop into gear more easily."

717

Car buyers could specify coloured seatbelts to match the exterior paint of their new Ferrari 458. This optional extra would have cost them £750.

718

The series of lights at the starting line in drag racing that count down to the start are often called 'the Christmas tree'.

719

When a large Royal Mail lorry hit the side of a VW Golf on the busy A40 in London, England, the trucker didn't realise. So he continued driving, pushing the Golf along in front of him, unseen beneath his elevated cockpit.

Amazingly, the first passing motorist on the scene was pop singer Ellie Goulding. She stopped and shouted at the lorry: "Oi, mate, you've got a car on you!"

He stopped and the car driver was rescued. Amazingly there were no injuries and no-one was charged. The Golf driver later messaged his thanks to the millionaire singer.

720 - 735

15 popular names for the Volkswagen Type 1

- o   Bug (USA)
- o   Beetle (UK)
- o   Tortoise Car (Nigeria)
- o   Kafer (Germany)
- o   Pulga or 'flea' (Columbia)
- o   Vocho or 'navel' (Mexico)
- o   Sapito or 'little toad' (Peru)
- o   Boblen or 'bubble' (Denmark)
- o   Coccinelle or 'ladybug' (France)
- o   Katsariaki or 'little cockroach' (Greece)
- o   Kodok or 'frog' (Indonesia)
- o   Foxy (Pakistan)
- o   Garbus or 'hunchback' (Poland)
- o   Volky (Puerto Rico)
- o   Burburuza or 'ladybird' (Romania)

735 - 738
Three other cars with nicknames
Model T Ford – Tin Lizzie
Subaru Impreza – Scooby
1932 Ford – Deuce Coupe

739

A 40-year-old male drunk driver was caught in Staffordshire, UK after blasting the police car in front with his horn… because he thought they were driving too slowly.

740

The Ford Capri was produced between 1968 and 1986, selling 1.9 models and achieving cult status in the UK. It was a two-door coupe designed as the European answer to the Ford Mustang and was mostly based on the mechanicals of the Cortina saloon. Ford's slogan was 'The car you always promised yourself'… Car magazine meanwhile called it "the Ford Cortina in drag."

741 - 768

A major study of all new cars was undertaken by European consumer magazine Which? Investigators looked for the cars with the worst visibility for drivers, using a 360-degree camera, ratings for headlights, mirrors and on-board technology. The worst score was 2 out of 5, which was shared by these 27 cars:

> Chevrolet Camaro
> Chevrolet Cruse
> Chevrolet Orlando
> Citroen Dispatch Combi Jumpy
> Citroen SpaceTourer
> Dacia Duster
> Dacia Sandero
> Ford Ecosport
> Ford Ka+
> Ford Ka+ Active
> Honda Civic
> Honda CR-Z
> Jeep Wrangler
> Kia Rio
> Mercedes GLC Coupe
> Nissan 370Z
> Nissan Micra
> Renault Fluence
> Renault Megane
> Renault Megane Coupe
> Renault Wind
> Smart EQ Fourtwo
> Smart Fortwo Cabriolet
> Toyota iQ
> Vauxhall Vivaro Life
> Volkswagen Jetta

769

Over 55s are much more likely to buy a car in cash (around 72% of them do this) than younger age groups.

770

A car conversion specialist in Maryland, USA, is producing its version of the Corvette ZR1… with the engine replaced by an electric motor. Genovation's GXE has 800bhp of emission-free power and a top speed of 220mph/354kph – making it one of the world's fastest electric cars.

771

Daewoo was a South Korean car-maker that rapidly rose to prominence in the 1980s. Its name meant 'The Great Woo' – referring to Kim Woo Choong, its founder. Sadly the great Woo oversaw an equally rapid decline in the company's fortunes and by 1999 it had collapsed. He was sentenced to ten years' jail for financial offences and his $22bn (£17bn) fortune was confiscated.

772

A study of 500,000 safety-related complaints about new American cars found that the most complained about model was the Chrysler 300, while the least complained about was the Kia Forte.

773

In his biography, Britain's most successful Touring Car driver Jason Plato revealed he was once arrested and spent a night in custody after trying to steal a JCB digger in the early hours in the glamorous city of Monte Carlo. "I was just trying to dig a hole," he explained.

774

Romanian car manufacturer Dacia unveiled its first ever concept car at the 2009 Geneva Motor Show. The innovative compact SUV featured a unique seating arrangement. The passenger seat could fold and slide under the driver's seat, and one rear seat could slide under the other. This created a long space precisely designed to transport a bicycle (according to a spokesman at the time). Sadly the car was never produced.

775 - 786

Another recent survey of cars that lose their value quickly. This time What Car? experts judged the ten UK cars that have the lowest trade-in value compared to their new price after three years ownership.

10 Citroen C3 (from £18,600 new to £5,100 trade-in)
9 Fiat Panda (£10,255 to £2,800)
8 Mercedes S-Class Cabriolet (£124,975 to £33,400)
7 Mercedes AMG E53 (£68,250 to £18,175)
6 Citroen C1 (£12,375 to £3,250)
5 Fiat 500C (£15,315 to £3,975)
4 Peugeot 108 (£13,670 to £3,425)
3 Maserati Quattroporte (£75,700 to £17,875)
2 Fiat Tipo (£20,385 to £4,625)
1 Peugeot 308 (£21,765 to £4,775)

787

In 1958 Citroen made a Sahara version of its 2CV which had two engines under the front seats. One drove the front wheels, the other the back wheels. The car came with two ignition keys and operated as a primitive form of four-wheel drive. It could be used as front-wheel drive or rear-wheel drive too. It cost £715 ($905) – double a standard 2CV - but Citroen sold 700.

788

Multi-millionaire Fiat owner Gianni Agnelli could order his car company to build him any car he wanted and had a sequence of one-off specials in his garage. They included a unique convertible version of the Lancia Delta Integrale and a three-seater Ferrari Testarossa.
One of his favourites, however, was a five-door family estate version created from the Fiat 130 saloon and fitted with a big, smooth 3.0-litre six-cylinder engine. Agnelli had a custom-made wicker roof box fitted to hold his skis and kept the car at his luxury mountain retreat at St Moritz in the Alps. The unique luxury car was only ever used to drive from the house... to the nearby ski lift.

789

A driver who crashed into a police car in Leicester, UK, then ran from the scene left an important clue behind... his baby. The fugitive was captured a short distance away and taken into custody. Meanwhile Twitter users ridiculed his actions.
"What was going to be their next move? "Oh hi, I was wondering if someone had handed a baby in?"' suggested one.

790 - 800

According to official **DVSA** figures these are the most durable high-mileage cars in the UK. The numbers refer to the cars still on the road that have recorded more than 250,000 miles.

- o Skoda Octavia - 1,950 models
- o Volkswagen Passat - 1,874 models
- o Toyota Prius - 1,742 models
- o Ford Mondeo - 1,278 models
- o Volkswagen Golf - 1,047 models
- o Toyota Avensis - 1,027 models
- o Audi A4 - 997 models
- o Mercedes Benz E-Class - 956 models
- o Ford Galaxy - 899 models
- o Audi A6 - 637 models

801

A unique Breitling dashboard clock could be specified when ordering a new Bentley Bentayga. This optional extra cost an additional £132,000.

Chapter 20

From the winning hairdresser...
To cheating in the backseat

802

Intrepid Italian driver Maria Teresa de Filippis was the first
woman to break into the staunchly male world of Formula
One racing.

- At the 1958 French Grand Prix at Reims, she was
  unable to compete after the French race director told
  her: "The only helmet a woman should wear is the one
  at the hairdresser's".
- Nevertheless in her debut in the 1958 Belgian Grand
  Prix she used extra padding on the back of the driver's
  seat so she could reach the pedals and went on to
  finish a creditable 10th.

803

In the sixties Ford originally tried to call its forthcoming
coupe the 'Colt' to show it was the European version of
the famous Mustang muscle car. Mitsubishi objected
because it already used the name and Ford was forced to
rename the new car at the last moment... as the Capri.

804

Research undertaken by America's Division of Trauma, Critical Care and Acute Care Surgery found there was 6.3% rise in the number of speed-related crashes following a televised motor sport race like Formula One or NASCAR.

805

Office worker Jason Walker from Crawley, Sussex, UK, who failed his driving test 11 times and wrote off his instructor's car by hitting a lamppost at speed while practising a three-point turn, finally passed in 2006.

806

Auto research website CarGurus recently found that British drivers' most wished-for rare dream car was a Chevrolet Camaro.

807

American footballer Odell Beckham Jr had the 'Spirit of Ecstasy' figure removed from the bonnet of his orange Rolls-Royce Cullinan. Instead the NFL receiver fitted a custom-made statuette... of himself making a great football catch.

808

The UK DVLA authority revealed that a classic car dealer paid £518,000 ($656,000) for the registration plate '25 O' when it was auctioned in 2014. It was then fitted to a Ferrari 250GT worth £10 million ($12.6m).

809 – 819

When AutoExpress magazine readers voted for the UK's worst ever cars, they chose:

10 Vauxhall Frontera
9 FSO Polonez
8 Reliant Robin
7 Morris Marina
6 Rover Cityrover
5 Alfa Romeo Arna
4 Ssangyong Rodius
3 Chrysler Cruiser Convertible
2 Austin Allegro
1 Revai G-Whiz

820

Travelling by car during peak periods is 13 times cheaper than taking the train in the UK, according to a report at thesun.co.uk.

821

In 1974 the Dacia factory in the Communist state of Romania launched its most up-market model to date, based on a sixties Renault 8. The 1301 Lux Super offered a 'lux' specification including a heated rear screen, door mirrors and a radio. Of course this highly luxurious vehicle was only available for Communist Party officials.

822

Around 50 million people a year around the world are injured in road accidents.

823

When American motoring organisation iseecars.com looked at 2.5 million vehicle ownership records they found that the ten cars that are held on to the longest by owners are all Japanese (the list included five Toyotas, three Hondas, one Lexus and one Subaru).

Even when they narrowed the study down to only look at pick-up trucks, the top five longest-lasting vehicles were still all Japanese.

824

As this book was being prepared BMW invested in an innovative Californian-based scheme to find a way of capturing CO_2 from the air and then using it as an eco-friendly fuel that could power existing vehicles.

825

The Cannonball Run is an illegal unofficial driving speed record route right across USA, coast-to-coast from New York City to Los Angeles.

The fastest time for the 2,825-mile (4,546km) challenge is currently 26 hours 38 minutes, set in April 2020. The average speed was 106mph (171kph). The team used an Audi A8L with extra fuel tanks and a nationwide system of police and traffic spotters. The record drive was posted on social media but, because of the speeds involved, the participants remained anonymous.

826 - 827

Czechoslovak car-maker Tatra launched the innovative 97 fastback saloon in 1936, with an air-cooled rear-mounted flat-four engine driving the rear wheels. In neighbouring Germany Adolf Hitler liked the design and announced: "This is the car for my roads."

Ferdinand Porsche appeared to copy the 97 to create the Volkswagen Beetle and please Hitler. His 'new' car also was a fastback saloon with an air-cooled rear-mounted flat-four engine driving the rear wheels.

Tatra sued but Hitler said he "would settle the matter". Soon after, his Nazi Germany invaded Moravia where the Tatra works were sited. The Nazis took over the Tatra factory and converted it to produce tank engines.

- After the war the Beetle became one of the world's most popular cars and Tatra tried to sue VW again. Eventually, in 1961, VW paid the now-Communist-state-owned Tatra 3 million Marks compensation, around £5m/$6.5m today.

828

Researchers watched hundreds of cars at road crossings across America and found drivers of less expensive cars are much more likely to stop for pedestrians than drivers of expensive cars. The journal of Transport & Health found no link to gender or race but the greatest predictor of whether a car would stop was its value.

829

In 1971 Ford built a one-off version of a van... with the underpinnings of a GT40 supercar. The Mark One Transit was secretly powered by a 5-0-litre V8 engine and first appeared at Brands Hatch race track as a promotional gimmick. The apparently normal white delivery van shocked onlookers by suddenly demonstrating its top speed of 168mph (270kph).

830 - 832

The simple Austin A-Series engine launched in 1951 was crude by today's standards, with an iron block, four cylinders and overhead valves operated by pushrods. It first powered the Austin A30, a small family car that had a 0-60mph time of 42.3seconds and a top speed of 67mph.

Yet this basic engine became one of the most influential in the modern era. Firstly it appeared in various forms in many British cars until 2000, including the Morris Minor, Mini, Austin Healey Sprite, Austin Metro, Austin Allegro, A40, Austin 1100/1300, Riley Elf, Wolsey Hornet, MG Midget, Lotus Seven, Morris Marina, Morris Ital, Austin Maestro, Austin Montego. An estimated 12 million cars used the engine.

- In addition, a diesel version of the A-Series was created and used in tractors and boats.
- And Nissan licensed the A-Series engine and created its own 'Nissan A Engine', which appeared in the Sunny, Pulsar, the Datsun Cherry, and various vans and pickups. The A Engine was also used in Premier sedans made in India.

833

Fire-fighters rushed to a cottage in a village in Wiltshire, England, early in 2020, to free an elderly woman trapped in the driver's seat after she had accidentally backed her car through her own front door into the hallway.

834

Seven different fuels used to power cars:
Petrol, diesel, electric, steam, jet, hydrogen, solar

835 - 843

Since cars were invented people have tried to create records by cramming as many humans inside various vehicles as possible.

Here are eight of the oddest records:

- o 25 German cheerleaders in an Audi A3 (2013)
- o 21 members of Plymouth Young Wives Association (UK) in a BL Metro (1982)
- o 12 healthcare professionals in Denver, USA, in a Buick LeSabre (2013)
- o 86 technology students, Carlow, Ireland, in a VW Campervan (2009)
- o 42 majorettes, Jacksonville, USA, in a Jaguar XJ6 (1984)
- o 354 Staffordshire schoolchildren in a double-decker London bus (1989)
- o 12 German men over 6'7" tall in a Trabant 601 (2000)
- o 30 Austrian youth club members in a VW Golf (1983)

844

The Sultan of Brunei (a tiny state on an island in southeast Asia with huge oil reserves) has the world's largest car collection. The sultan has more than 7,000 cars, estimated to be worth $2.3 trillion/£1.8 trillion.

He is known for taking things to extremes, even his name is extreme. In full he calls himself: Kebawah Duli Yang Maha Mulia Paduka Seri Baginda Sultan Haji Hassanal Bolkiah Mu'izzaddin Waddaulah ibni Al-Marhum Sultan Haji Omar 'Ali Saifuddien Sa'adul Khairi Waddien, Sultan dan Yang Di-Pertuan Negara Brunei Darussalam.

'Keb's' car collection includes a custom Rolls Royce stretch limo plated in 24-carat gold, two Ferrari Mythos concept cars, 80 Bentley Turbo Rs and Ferrari 456 GTs (in various different colours), 134 Koenigsegg supercars, the only Mercedes CLK GTR track car with right-hand drive, six of the nine Ferrari FXs ever built, a one-off 1934 Rolls Royce called 'The Star of India' valued at $14million, all three of the only Aston Martin V8 Vantage Specials ever built, and ten custom-built Mercedes estates each with a 7.3-litre V12 engine.

845

In 1904 the pioneering Ladies Automobile Club held its first event, in the heart of London. The Duchess of Sutherland led a procession of 56 women and their cars along Pall Mall, as Queen Alexandra watched the brave ladies from the window at Buckingham Palace. Many of the women drove themselves… but some sat in the passenger seat smiling and relied on their male chauffeurs to actually do the job of piloting the cars.

846

A quarter of under-34 year olds in the UK spend more on monthly payments for their car than on their rent or mortgage on their home.

847 - 848

Stirling Moss was a famous British motor racer with 16 Grand Prix victories. Less well-known is that his sister Pat Moss was a very successful rally driver, winning three international rallies and being was five-time European Ladies Rally Champion.

- *Pat Moss married Swedish rally star Erik Carlsson, Rally Hall of Fame inductee who was so famous for his exploits in Saabs they named a car after him.*

849

In a recent survey 25% of motorists claim to have cheated on their partners in a car.

Chapter 21
From a Monte Carlo marathon…
To a budget Popemobile

850

Intrepid motoring pioneer Joan Richmond overcame a
tough handicap compared to all the other entrants in the
1932 Monte Carlo Rally… she drove her car all the way
from Australia to get there.

Nevertheless Joan finished 17th in her Riley 9.

851 - 856

A survey of 200 English Premier League footballers found the five players with the most expensive cars

- Pierre-Emerick Aubameyang (Arsenal) – Ferrari LaFerrari £1,150,000
- Heung-Min Son (Tottenham) – Ferrari LaFerrari £1,150,000
- Paul Pogba (Manchester United) – McLaren P1 £866,000
- Roberto Firmino (Liverpool) – Rolls Royce Phantom £360,000
- Dele Alli (Tottenham) – Rolls Royce Phantom £360,000

857 – 862

The five players with the least expensive cars were

- Lewis Cook (Bournemouth) - VW Scirocco £20,533
- Angelo Ogbonna (West Ham) - Fiat Freemont £23,342
- N'Golo Kante (Chelsea) – Mini Cooper £23,395
- Andrew Surman (Bournemouth) – Mercedes AMG A-Class £26,155
- Solly March (Brighton) - Mercedes AMG A-Class £26,155

863 - 865

Online car-parts distributor Mister Auto conducted an extensive survey of driving conditions in cities around the world, taking into account traffic congestion, road quality, driving culture and safety, pollution, costs, and incidents of road rage.

The top ten cities were

1 Calgary, Canada

2 Dubai, UAE

3 Ottawa, Canada

4 Bern, Switzerland

5 El Paso, USA

6 Vancouver, Canada

7 Gothenburg, Sweden

8 Dusseldorf, Germany

9 Basel, Switzerland

10 Dortmond, Germany

(London was 77th, Los Angeles 78th, New York 87th)

866

The world's worst ten cities for driving (worst first) were

1 Mumbai, India

2 Ulaanbaatar, Mongolia

3 Kolkata, India

4 Lagos, Nigeria

5 Karachi, Pakistan

6 Bogota, Columbia

7 Sao Paulo, Brazil

8 Mexico City, Mexico

9 Rio de Janeiro, Brazil

10 Moscow, Russia

867

Garmin has released a rear-facing bike-radar system that warns pedal cyclists of a car approaching by flashing an alert on a special high-tech handlebar-mounted display.

868

Bugatti teamed with luxury jeweller Jacob & Co to produce a very limited edition super-watch to celebrate the Chiron becoming the world's fastest production car. Only three of the carbon and titanium Twin Turbo 300+ watches were made and they cost more than many supercars: a cool $580,000/£412,000 each.

869 - 870

The 2020 JD Power 'Initial Quality Survey' in the US recorded buyers reactions to their new cars after exactly 90 days of ownership. It showed that price and prestige were no guarantee of quality.

- Highest rated brands were
  1 Dodge
  2 Kia
  3 Chevrolet
  4 Ram
  5 Genesis

- Lowest rated brands were (worst first)
  1 Tesla
  2 Land Rover
  3 Audi
  4 Volvo
  5 Mercedes

871

In 1965 Peugeot shocked petrol devotees by building a one-off single-seater diesel version of its 404 family car purely to break track records and show off the potential of diesel engines.

The light-blue 404 racer had a 2.0-litre, 69bhp, non-turbo engine and drove 3,100 miles (5,000km) flat-out almost non-stop for 72 hours at Monthlery circuit near Paris. The feat needed a team of five drivers and was completed at an average speed of 99mph (159kph).

872

Here's another Peugeot story: If you type the wrong address or a broken link on the Peugeot website, instead of a standard '404 Error message' you are taken to a photo of a Peugeot 404.

873

A study of vehicle depreciation according to car colour, conducted by iseecars.com, found that yellow cars hold their value best, while gold cars lose more value than any other colour.

874 - 876

The Aston Martin Bulldog of 1980 was a one-off futuristic prototype that was abandoned during one of the company's frequent changes of ownership.

The wedge-shaped supercar had powered gull-wing doors, five headlights in a row across the middle of the bonnet and a twin-turbo V8 that powered it to 200mph (320kph)... so it would have been the world's fastest production car at the time.

- In 1983 VW built a one-off version of its Scirocco coupe... with two engines. Each 2.0-litre unit powered one of the axles. The model was tested up to 180mph and was designed as an answer to the growing vogue for four-wheel drive.
- The following year Lancia experimented with the same idea and built a four-door Trevi saloon with two turbocharged engines. It had a sort-of-four-wheel-drive and lots of power but the car needed it – because the two lots of engines and the car's mechanicals weighed so much.

877

Italian supercar manufacturer Lamborghini demonstrated the enormous vanity at the heart of all supercar ownership on its own 50th birthday.

It built a one-off supercar called the Egoista (Italian for egotistical) in 2013. The exotic 5.2-litre carbonfibre and aluminium coupe wasn't sold; Lamborghini kept it for itself and it is now in the marque's museum.

Appropriately, the Egoista had only one seat.

878 - 888

The ultimate global motorsport events to watch

(From autocar.co.uk)

1 Monte Carlo Rally (France) - "on the edge of chaos"

2 Daytona 500 (Florida, USA) - "intense pack racing"

3 Nurburgring 24 Hours (Germany) – "as hairy as legend dictates"

4 Spa 6 Hours (Belgium) – "old school"

5 Bathurst 1000 (Australia) – "big, brash, spectacular"

6 Macau Grand Prix – "crash-bang-wallop street circuit"

7 Pikes Peak (Colorado, USA) – "world's toughest hillclimb"

8 Indy 500 (Indiana, USA) – "exceeds its hype"

9 Le Mans 24 Hours (France) – "forget about sleep"

10 British Grand Prix – "electric atmosphere"

889 – 891

The DUKW is probably the world's most famous amphibious motor vehicle. The six-wheel-drive personnel or cargo-carrier was produced from 1942 by General Motors, with underpinnings based on its GMC truck.

With its hefty waterproof panels the DUKW weighed more than six tonnes and only used a 4.0-litre, 91bhp, straight-six engine. Yet the 'Duck' was capable of 50mph (80kph) on land and 6.5mph (10kph) on water.

The driver simply moved a gearlever to select propeller power. They were used in World War II, the Korean War and Vietnam. British Royal Marines kept a small force of DUKWs in service until 2012.

Around the world they can still be seen offering tourist rides in cities with rivers, like London and Hong Kong.

- o The DUKW was an unlikely pioneer of motoring technology. It was the first production vehicle to allow the driver to alter the tyre pressure from their seat. DUKW pilots could inflate tyres for hard surfaces like concrete or reduce pressure to cross beach sand.

- o In 1973 Martin Buchanan crossed the Irish Sea (37miles/59km) in a VW Beetle he had converted to be amphibious. He sailed from the Isle of Man to Blackpool, taking a little under eight hours. Buchanan dramatically ran out of fuel before reaching the shore but managed to drift onto the beach using the current.

892 - 899

A 'sleeper' or 'Q-Car' is slang for a car that has an unassuming exterior... but is capable of very high performance. (Sleeper agents were inactive secret agents in foreign states awaiting instructions to begin spying while Q-Ships were Royal Navy gunboats disguised as merchant navy vessels).

Here are seven examples of Q Cars
- Chrysler 300D (1958) - the luxury four-seater was first production car with more 300bhp
- Lotus Cortina (1963) - had a racing engine in a top-selling family car
- Mercedes 300 SEL 6.3 (1968) - the large sober limousine was world's fastest saloon
- Lancia Thema (1986) – a four-door family saloon with a Ferrari V8 engine
- Lotus Carlton (1990) – executive barge tuned to reach 177mph (285mph)
- Mazda 6 MPS (2005) – all-wheel-drive high-performance hidden under standard saloon body
- Tesla Model S P100D Ludicrous (2017) – supercar-beating acceleration in eco-car

900

During an official visit to Abu Dhabi, Pope Francis had no popemobile available - so had to be driven around waving at crowds in a Kia Soul hatchback.

Chapter 22

From flops to fantasy
Some lists of trivia

901 - 919

The 18 biggest flops in automotive history

(According to autocar.co.uk)

1 Tucker 1948

This technically advanced, rear-engined fastback sedan was independently produced and marketed across the US. Only 51 were sold.

2 Ford Edsel 1958

An enormous marketing campaign failed to sell the quirky up-market newcomer and it was dropped within two years. Ford lost $350 million (£268m).

3 Citroen Bijou 1960

A cramped glass-fibre-bodied coupe version of the 2CV built in Slough for UK buyers sold precisely 207 models.

4 Bricklin SV-1 1974

'Safety Vehicle One' wasn't the sexiest name for this Canadian gull-wing 6.0-litre sports coupe… and eventually less than 3,000 were built.

5 DeLorean DMC-2 1981

Debts, drug-scandals and the peak of the Northern Irish troubles doomed the exciting stainless steel sportscar brand to a loss-making 8,583 sales.

6 Alfa Romeo Arna 1984

Alfa's version of the Nissan Cherry created a badly built dull hatchback that was quickly dropped after 61,750 global sales.

7 Rover Sterling 1987

British luxury and Japanese tech combined to tackle the US market but rust and reliability issues punctured the dream. Rover never returned to the US.

8 Jaguar XJ220 1992

The 213mph (343kph) supercar launched into a recession and had to be sold at a loss, just to shift the 274 they built.

9 GM EV1 1996

Ugly pioneering electric coupe was leased, not sold. Just over 1,000 were built, most were crushed.

10 Cadillac Catera 1996

Ater five years trying to sell these re-badged Vauxhall Omegas in America only 95,000 customers had been found.

11 Plymouth Prowler 1997

Chrysler's retro hot-rod was an acquired taste that only 11,702 buyers acquired. When it died, so did the Plymouth brand.

12 Pontiac Aztek 2000

Hideous crossover SUV was produced for seven years before the axe and in none of those did it make a profit.

13 Renault Avantime 2001

Weird coupe version of Espace was brave and unusual… but was canned after just two years and 8,500 sales.

14 Chrysler Crossfire 2003

This odd coupe offspring of German Mercedes and American Chrysler disappeared after its parents divorced.

15 Tata Nano 2008

The Indian-built four-seater city car cost just £1900/$2500 and aimed to revolutionise the country's transport. Seven years later Tata pulled the plug after disappointing sales.

16 Acura ZDX 2009

'Distinctive' looks, suicidal visibility and thirsty engines restricted this crossover coupe to 7,191 sales in four years.

17 Saab 9-5 2010

The bulbous, dated, third-generation 9-5 was launched in the middle of corporate upheaval and soon disappeared forever.

18 Nissan Murano CrossCabriolet 2011

An over-priced two-door open-top 4WD SUV was not the answer to anyone's question. It was 'phased out' with no replacement by 2014.

920 - 925

Five quotes from five-time world champion racing driver Juan Manuel Fangio

o "You must always believe you will become the best, but you must never believe you have done so."

o "There is a formula for success, and it is not difficult to analyse. It is made up of 50 per cent car, 25 per cent driver and 25 per cent luck."

o "If I were really rich, I would ask myself: 'What for?' I enjoy myself more than others who have made materialism their maxim."

o "When one runs the risk of losing a sense of proportion, it's time to go home, sleep in the same bed in which one dreamed while still a nobody, and to eat the simple, healthy dishes of one's childhood."

o "To race is to live. But those who died while racing knew, perhaps, how to live more than all the others."

926 – 933

The seven ugliest Ferraris of all time

(Courtesy autowise.com)

For many years Ferrari allowed coach builders to create unique bodies for clients, sometimes resulting in truly awful designs with the Ferrari name. In descending order here are the worst:

- 1966 Ferrari 330GT 2+2 'Navarro' (Drogo)
  Hideous design disaster commissioned by Italian nightclub boss featuring a drooping elongated nose and two tail fins
- 1993 Ferrari FZ93 (Zagato)
  Laughably bad effort with a double-bubble roof, two-tone paint-job, red wheels and big black horse motifs on side panels
- Ferrari 308 GT4 Rainbow (Bertone)
  Unsurprisingly this angular Thunderbirds-are-go styling was Bertone's last employment by Ferrari
- 1983 Ferrari 400i Meera S (Michelotti)
  Built for an Arab Prince, and with the unique feature of side window wipers, it was likened to an RX-7 kit car replica
- 2006 Ferrari 575 GTZ (Zagato)
  A run of six aluminium bodied specials shared the two-tone grey colour scheme and apparently the front end of a fifties Corvette
- 1965 Ferrari 330 'Shooting Brake' (Vignale)
  One of the ugliest cars ever designed, the cartoon-like Ferrari estate looks at its absolute worst in the official yellow and turquoise colour scheme
- 1956 Ferrari Superamerica 410 (Ghia)
  So bad it's almost desirable. But not quite. The 410 featured huge tail fins, a heavy chrome strip from tiny front headlights to rear bumper, bull-bar front bumper and bonnet featuring scoops, dips, ridges and wings

934 – 940
Six slogans from 1981 DeLorean brochure

DE LOREAN
The man, the company, the car

DE LOREAN
The next generation

DE LOREAN
Distinctive looks from any direction

DE LOREAN
Engineered for total performance

DE LOREAN
Matchless detail for comfort and convenience

DE LOREAN
Where it all comes together

941 - 946

Five cars named after fish

- o Corvette Sting Ray
- o Open Manta
- o AMC Marlin
- o Plymouth Barracuda
- o Hyundai Tiburon (Spanish for shark)

947 - 959

12 cars named after mammals

- o Ford Puma
- o Chevrolet Impala
- o VW Fox
- o Singer Gazelle
- o Jaguar
- o Ford Mustang
- o Ford Pinto
- o VW Rabbit
- o Dodge Ram
- o Triumph Stag
- o Buick Wildcat
- o Ford Cougar

960 - 965

Five cars named after insects

- o VW Beetle
- o Hudson Wasp
- o Dodge SuperBee
- o Alfa Romeo Spider
- o Datsun Honey Bee

966

Two cars named after snakes

- o Dodge Viper
- o AC Cobra

967

Four cars named after magical creatures

- o Riley Elf
- o Ford Thunderbird
- o Pontiac Firebird
- o AMC Gremlin

Chapter 23

From taming The Beast of Turin…
To a quick way to get rid of a beard

968 - 969

The extraordinary Fiat S76 of 1910 had a petrol engine with only four cylinders… but an enormous displacement of 28.3-litres (1,730cu in). Contemporaries nicknamed the huge Fiat 'The Beast of Turin'.

This 28,300cc engine took up most of the car, with just a small two-seater open cockpit behind. Its unusual technical configuration included three spark plugs per cylinder, a chain-operated gearbox and crude leaf-spring suspension.

- *Italian race driver Felice Nazzaro tested the first S76 and judged it "uncontrollable". The second was sold to Russian Prince Boris Soukanhov, who hired a sequence of rather reluctant professional racing drivers to try it. Eventually moustachioed New Yorker Arthur Duray, an early aviation pioneer, managed to control the Prince's car and reach the speed of 132.27mph (213kph) on Ostende Beach in Belgium in December 2013. This achievement meant that 'The Beast' had set a new world land speed record.*

970

In 2020 English teacher Nigel Wright was fined £100 for stopping for 35 seconds outside East Midlands airport car park while he waited for the barrier to rise to let him in. Officials claimed he was in a 'no stopping zone'.

971

A driver who filmed himself laughing as he drove through the streets of Barcelona at 125mph with one hand on the wheel and the other doing a thumbs up, posted it on Instagram... and was promptly tracked down by Spanish police through his account and prosecuted.

972

Australia's best-known motoring marque, Holden, was originally a 19th-century saddler-maker. Then the company started making leather seats for horse-drawn carriages and later moved into motor vehicle interiors too. By 1914 Holden began making its own cars and ending up dominating the Australian car industry.
The marque had sold 8 million cars since the Second World War when parent company General Motors decided to close it down in 2017.

973

Manchester police used an unmarked truck to film motorists in 2017 ...and were horrified to spot drivers playing with iPads, watching TV and eating pot noodles while at the wheel.

974

How to do a doughnut in a car

(A doughnut is a showing-off skidding pirouette)

(From Carthrottle.com)

1) **Drive around a cone**

   Pop it in first gear, drive around the cone in a circle, almost on full steering lock. Keep going faster until you feel the front starting to slip.

2) **Lift your foot off the accelerator**

   Once the front starts to slip take your foot off the accelerator to shift all the weight to the front of the car, leaving the back of the car feeling light (lift-off oversteer).

3) **Get back on the accelerator**

   Once you've felt the weight shift (made visible by a passenger's head falling forward) get back on the accelerator, foot to the floor. This will spin the rear wheels and they will start sliding the back of the car towards the outside of the circle.

4) **Let go of the steering wheel and reduce the amount of acceleration**

   Once the back starts to step out, let go of the steering wheel and let it turn onto opposite lock. Reduce the accelerator to about half at the same time. Depending on set-up, some cars need some encouragement to get onto opposite lock.

5) **Grab the steering wheel and slide gracefully around the cone**

   Once the back of the car is so far sideways that the nose of the car is more or less facing the cone, grab hold of the steering wheel and use minor adjustments to the throttle to control the angle of the car, navigating in a circle around the cone. More power will tighten the circle, less gets you running wider.

975

**A survey in 2018 found the average driver swears
once every two-and-a-half miles.**

976

In 1989 Japanese manufacturer Isuzu revealed a stunning
concept car at the Tokyo Motor Show. The mid-engined
4200R coupe was way ahead of its time with four seats, active
suspension and sat-nav. Enthusiasts eagerly awaited the car's
launch - when suddenly Isuzu bosses stopped all car
development work to focus purely on commercial vehicles.
The 4200R was never seen again.

977

*A couple from England's northeast who bought a new VW Tiguan in
2017 took it back to the dealership… complaining that the sat-nav
system didn't pronounce local place names correctly.*

978

Italian racing driver Alex Zanardi had a successful career in
Formula One and won the CART World Championship Series
twice, before a terrible crash in 2001 in which he lost both legs.
Amazingly he returned to motorsport and within two years was
winning races in the World Touring Car Championships. If
that wasn't enough, Zanardi also took up paralympic cycling,
using his hands to turn the pedals. He became the best in the
world, winning four Olympic golds and two silvers.
Tragically Zanardi suffered another crash, this time in his
hand-cycle in 2020. At the time of writing he remains in a very
serious condition with severe head injuries in hospital but
seems to be recovering slowly.

979 - 980

In 2007 two Wrangler Jeeps spent five days driving up the rocky slopes and ice fields to the top of Ojos del Salado, a 6,646 meter/21,804ft volcano in the Andes as a promotional stunt for Chrysler.

- *In 2021 the Chief of the Cherokee Nation asked Chrysler to stop using Cherokee as the model name of its best-selling SUV. "It's part of our identity," he complained. Jeep replied that the name had been used for 45 years and was chosen "to honour and celebrate Native American people for their nobility, prowess and pride."*

981

When Kia went bust in 1997 Samsung tried to buy it... but was outbid by Hyundai.

982

Esteemed American motoring pioneer William C Durant, who founded General Motors, had a bizarre middle name that dated back to his mother's French family.
His full name was William Crapo Durant.

983

The GMC Hummer EV is a large off-road electric vehicle planned by General Motors at the time of writing this book. Its launch was delayed by the coronavirus pandemic. The 1,000bhp SUV is claimed to accelerate from 0-60mph (97kph) in just three seconds.

984 - 987

After World War Two, former Irish Guardsman Archie Butterworth, who had become famous for shooting down a German plane with a pistol, designed and built his own four-wheel-drive racing car for £300 ($375).

The AJB Special was powered by an old Steyr 4.4-litre V8 engine from a German half-track mounted into a stiffened Jeep chassis with four-wheel drive. Butterworth devised his own optimum mix of methanol, benzole and petrol for the AJB Special and started racing in 1948. At first it had no brakes so Butterworth would slow down by simply stretching out and using his hands on the rear tyres.

Careful tuning raised the output to 260bhp, similar to a contemporary Ferrari racing car and Butterworth entered an F1 race in 1950. It was the first four-wheel-drive F1 entrant and it cornered on two wheels so the underside of the car became clearly visible.

The unusual car and its homespun driver became a favourite with crowds and achieved some successes in speed trials and hill climbs before a major crash in 1951.

- o   American fan Bill Milliken bought the wreck of the AJB Special and took it back to Buffalo, New York, where he rebuilt it as 'The Butterball Special'. Milliken raced it for five years, including setting a new track record at Holland Hill Climb.

- o   The Butterball Special ended up at the Four Wheel Drive Museum in Wisconsin where it is still displayed.

988

The fastest production Fiat of all time was the Fiat Coupe 2.0-litre 16v Turbo of 1997. The low two-door, two-seater sports car used a five-cylinder petrol engine to reach a top speed of 155mph (250kph). The distinctive lines of the Fiat supercoupe were not, however, the work of any of the big Italian design houses. The Coupe was designed by American Chris Bangle.

989

The most criticised car of all time is believed to be the Triumph Mayflower (1949-53), an attempt to create a small British luxury limousine for the American market. It had awkward proportions and was underpowered, with a top speed of just 63mph (101kph).

Top Gear/Grand Tour pundit James May called it the ugliest car ever built, saying: "Its details are ugly, its overall proportions are ugly, its very concept – as a car to appeal to Americans who believed they were directly descended from the Pilgrim Fathers – makes one shudder."

The Mayflower was also included in the list of 'Cars That Should Never Have Been Built' by Stuff.co.nz, which concluded: "It always looked like the misshapen out-of-scale miniature of the larger, more elegant Renown model, viewed in the distorted reflection of a fairground mirror."

The Mayflower was also featured in the books 'The Worst Cars Ever Sold' by Giles Chapman, 'Naff Motors: 101 Automotive Lemons' by Tony Davis and 'The World's Worst Cars' by Craig Cheetham, who said that it had: "The appearance of a Rolls-Royce Phantom that had been chopped in the middle."

990

How to take a gravel corner Dukes-of-Hazzard style
(From MensHealth.com)

"Going sideways is the quickest way through a corner on dirt", explained stunt driver Rhys Millen from seventies TV hit series Dukes of Hazzard.

Millen was the main driver of the starring car 'General Lee', a 1969 Dodge Charger that drifted and skidded more than it steered.

"To do it well," said Millen, "initiate the slide through input to the steering wheel. Oversteer into the turn, then flick the wheel in the opposite direction of the curve to break traction. Whip it back the other way to initiate a slide in the direction you want to go. Once the car starts to slide, you can 'steer' by adjusting the throttle. More or less throttle will make the car slide at a wider or tighter arc, respectively.

"More gas makes for a more sideways slide. If you lift off the throttle, the car will still go sideways, but it will start to reduce speed and straighten out again."

991

Motorway police on northern England's M6 stopped a driver when they spotted his wife in the boot of his car. The man had driven 100 miles to collect a window, which took up all the vehicle space. His wife was relegated to the boot for the return journey. Police issued a fixed penalty fine.

992

Honda is the largest engine manufacturer in the world. It makes more than 14 million engines a year.

993 - 994

One of the most recognisable logos in the world is Ford's blue oval, featuring a stylised version of Henry Ford's signature. The iconic symbol was created by a humble Ford design shop staff member using his grandfather's stencil set in 1907.

- Ford is the world's largest family-owned business.

995

In contrast to Ford, most car enthusiasts have never heard of Yazaki, a family-owned company based in Tokyo, Japan... but most production cars in the world wouldn't work without them. Yazaki is the world's leading supplier of automotive wiring harnesses, the electrical network behind the dashboard and controls. It also produces vast quantities of instrument clusters, displays and switches. Even though they are fierce business rivals, most of the major car manufacturers use Yazaki's products, including Toyota, Honda, GM, Ford, Fiat-Chrysler, Tesla, Subaru, Nissan, Mazda, Jaguar Land Rover and the PSA Group.

996

Former Swedish diplomat Bo Andersson became president of Russia's ailing GAZ car manufacturer in 2009 when it was losing $1 billion a year. Andersson scrapped the iconic GAZ Volga saloon, trimmed staff, introduced profit-sharing and eliminated corruption. Within two years GAZ had revenue of $4.1 billion and had made the biggest annual profit in its history. Andersson was promptly awarded the Adam Smith Institute's 'Automotive Executive of the Year' title.

997

Proud All-American brand Chevy re-badged the Japanese Toyota Corollas as its own 'Chevrolet Prizm' for 12 years from 1990.

998

Although the American Purple Heart award is usually only awarded to humans, a Jeep received one after it survived two beach landings during World War II.

999

In 1999 Mitsubishi introduced a mini people-carrier called the Toppo BJ. The BJ initials were later explained as standing for 'Big Joy'.

1000

The driver of a Seat hatchback cruising through the centre of Halifax, England, used "excessive' amounts of air freshener spray in his car... then lit a cigarette.

Yorkshire firefighters reported that the resulting explosion blew out all the windows and lights, and buckled the roof and doors.

Amazingly the driver escaped with minor injuries and later told reporters: "There was an almighty noise and a blinding light. I thought I'd been caught in a terror attack. It singed my hair and burnt my beard off."

Epilogue

Using up some left-overs…
Some are okay

1001

In 2020 the Daily Mail reported on a driver spotted by several customers at a filling station struggling to fill his car with petrol. The young male in shorts, sunglasses and a reversed baseball cap searched around his car for the filler cap, even looking inside the boot… seemingly unaware that the car he was driving was a Tesla S that runs on electric battery power. He was even seen trying to push the pump nozzle into the electric charging point. Finally the young driver appeared to check the details of the car on his phone, shook his head, and got in and drove away.

1002

Smart cars were promoted in a giant billboard campaign in some American states that referred to the city-car's tiny wheelbase, saying: "Save money. Share a parking meter."

1003

Jaguar workers brush the bare body shell of all their unpainted cars with an ionized emu feather. This is because the emu feather holds a high electrostatic charge and the process means that the bare metal won't attract dust between the cleaning and painting stage.

1004

Research has found that more than 200,000 tonnes of tiny plastic particles from tyres and brakes find their way in the world's oceans every year. Scientists found that an average tyre sheds 4kg of rubber during its lifetime.

1005

During the covid pandemic officials announced they would start showing films on a giant screen to cars parked in Brighton Station car park in the evening. The drive-in style movies would be shown at a time when there weren't many trains according to the officials.

1006

For some reason Americans don't like Suzukis. Because of poor sales, the tenth biggest car manufacturer in the world stopped selling new cars in the US in 2012... and hasn't sold one there since.

1007

In the 1984 Monaco Grand Prix a young unknown Brazilian driver in his first F1 season, driving an unfancied and uncompetitive Toleman, started at a lowly 13th on the grid. The conditions were shocking on the notorious street circuit but the newcomer drove like a man possessed.

He overtook the greatest drivers of the day, Rosberg, Piquet, Lauda, Arnoux and Mansell, and ended up in second place, with just race leader Alain Proust left to overcome... then the rain became so bad that the race was abandoned on the 31st lap.

The young driver was Ayrton Senna.

1008 - 1020

The Nash Metropolitan (1954 – 62) was America's first small car at less than 13ft long (10 inches smaller than a VW Beetle). Sadly the dainty British-built mini-car with whitewall tyres and built-in radio arrived at a time when the US fashion was for bigger cars. Sales were low and the car deemed a failure. It has since become a cult favourite. Here are 12 facts about it:

- Utility production ideas meant that the Metropolitan's two doors were identical: left and right-side doors were produced with the same pressing and are interchangeable
- Many underpinnings were shared with the Frog-Eyed Sprite and the engine with the MGA
- First year models had an air scoop in the bonnet. It was a fake that did nothing but attempt to look sporty
- The 1961 advert showed the car alongside a ballerina in a tutu holding waterskis
- Nash also made Kelvinator fridges
- It was the first American car specifically marketed to women. Its slogan was "The personal car for girls on the go"
- The convertible had such a small back seat the whole car was called a three-seater
- It was due to be called the 'NKI Custom' until just before launch. 'Metropolitan' badges had to be made to fit the same holes as the ditched name
- Two stationwagon prototypes were built and one is still housed in a California museum
- Only left-hand-drive versions were available for promotional photos so Austin simply reversed the photo for UK brochures
- Austin called it the 'Metro' in house and re-used the name for a small hatchback in 1980
- In 1960 Metropolitan gave Princess Margaret a black car with gold leather interior that was later stolen

1021

The Vector M12 was the worst supercar in history (according to drivetribe.com)

It was closely related to the Lamborghini Diablo and used the sister company's V12 engine… but poor sales meant only 17 were produced between 1995 and 1999, rather than the planned 150 a year. It is believed only 14 were sold. One was sold to tennis star Andre Agassi who quickly returned it after it broke down.

The handling, build, reliability, design and cramped interior all were criticised and when Autoweek tested the M12 it called it 'the worst car ever tested in the history of the magazine'.

1022

The 1932 Terraplane, built by Detroit's Hudson Motor Car Company, had a unique safety feature: "Duo-automatic brakes". The car was fitted with two braking systems, hydraulic and mechanical. If one failed, for example if the brakes pipes leaked, the mechanical brakes could be used to slow and stop the car.

- o The car's sales slogan was: "On the sea that's aquaplaning, in the air that's aeroplaning, but on the land, in the traffic, on the hills, hot diggity dog, THAT'S TERRAPLANING"

1023

Most manufacturers' use variable valve timing systems in their engines. They all pretend their system is unique and give it a different name. Here are some:

Honda VTEC
Citroen VTi
MG VVC
Nissan VVL
Audi Valvelift
Nissan VVEL
Toyota VVT-I
Chrysler/GM/VW VVT
Porsche VarioCam
Alfa Romeo VCT
BMW Vanos
Ford Ti-VCT
Mazda S-VT
Mitsubishi MIVEC
Daihatsu DVVT
Proton CPS
Subaru AVLS

1024

The Hyundai badge, featuring a slanted H in an oval, also represents two people shaking hands.

1025

A middle-aged driver was caught by traffic police and fined after he was spotted driving his VW Passat to a West Wales scrapyard in 2019... with a Skoda Octavia on top of his car, strapped to the roof.

1026 - 1031

Ford 1918 sales brochure (extracts)

"FORD – the universal car
In the beginning was the Ford car and the Ford car was right. Right in design and right in construction - a motor car to satisfactorily meet all the demands of the people for service and pleasure – the car for the multitudes.

"While there are nearly two hundred different makers of motor cars in America, the Ford factory produces more than one half of the entire aggregate output. One half of all the cars on American roads are Ford cars. It wouldn't be so universally in demand if it were not so universally good.

"All Ford cars will turn in a 28ft circle. This feature is of great advantage while operating in crowded thoroughfares.

"Ford springs are the strongest and most flexible that can be made.

"All Ford cars are sold completely equipped, except for a speedometer."

1032

Honda runs 280 farms in Ohio, growing soya beans, which are then exported back to Japan in the empty containers that originally brought car parts from the Far East to the factory in America.

1033 – 1040

Seven unusual types of car doors

- Butterfly doors: move up and out using hinges along the A pillar (1969 Alfa Romeo 33 Stradale and 1992 McLaren F1)

- Scissor doors: move straight up using single hinges at the top of the front wing (1974 Lamborghini Countach and 1990 Diablo)

- Gull-wing doors: hinged at the top (1952 Mercedes 300SL and 1981 DeLorean)

- Dihedral doors: rotate 90-degrees at the hinge (Koenigsegg supercars)

- Suicide doors: hinged at rear of door (Ford Thunderbird 1967 and Mazda RX-8)

- Swan doors: open normally but slightly upwards to clear curbs and obstructions (2003 Aston Martin DB9 and 2011 Hennessey Venom GT)

- Canopy door: whole cockpit roof and sides lift like aircraft (1953 Messerschmitt KR175 and 1970 Bond Bug)

- Sliding doors: side door opens by running along a track (Toyota Previa and Renault Kangoo)

1041

We won't go into the sub-category of 'pocket doors' where the door slides down into the bodywork of the car, or sideways in the 1954 Kaiser Darrin or right down into the chassis in the 1989 BMW Z1.

1042

Cars with no doors:
- Allard Clipper (1953)
- Ariel Atom (2000)
- Bond Minicar (1949)
- Brutsch Mopetta (1956)
- Goggomobil Dart (1959)
- Myers Manx (1964)
- Mini Moke (1964)
- VW Schwimmwagen (1941)
- Zenos E10 (2013)

1043

The 2011 Hyundai Veloster is unique because it has one door on the driver's side… and two on the passenger side.

1044

Enough doors. Wealthy American student Whitney Straight became a successful Grand Prix racing driver… while still an undergraduate student at Cambridge University in England. Fellow students in the thirties were amazed when Straight would rush from lectures to fly in a private plane to Brooklands Circuit to compete.

Chapter X

The last few dregs
Almost finished…

Some things about Le Mans:

1045

In the 1927 the winning margin between the first and second-placed cars at end of the Le Mans 24-hour race was the biggest ever… 217 miles (350km).

1046 - 1050

Four more stories about Le Mans

1) During the Le Mans 24-Hour endurance race conditions can get very difficult at night. With speeds of over 186mph/300kph in wet weather, visibility can be so poor, that despite marker boards along the track, drivers count in their heads along the straights in order to know when a corner is approaching.

2) There are also Le Mans 24-Hour endurance races for large trucks of more than 5.3 tons and for motorbikes.

3) The 1955 Le Mans disaster was one of motorsport's worst ever crashes. A French driver fatally crashed and so much debris flew into the crowd 83 spectators were killed and 180 injured.

4) During the 1984 Le Mans British driver John Sheldon crashed at more than 200mph (320kph), ripped through Armco barriers and exploded in the trees, killing a marshal and setting the wood on fire. Sheldon and two spectators were severely injured. His American team-mate Drake Olson then crashed into the debris and was also injured.

1051

Cycling weekly magazine reported how the driver of a Ferrari 488 Pista swerved to avoid a wobbly cyclist on the A25 in Surrey, England... and crashed into a tree, writing off his £250,000 car. The cyclist and Ferrari driver were unharmed but the car was left with branches protruding from the windows.

1052

The driver of a $250,000 McLaren 600LT supercar was caught on video trying to drive through a flooded stretch of road in South Carolina, USA after recent freak rainfall. The driver lost all control as his low-slung coupe started floating. The car was seen simply sailing away into the vegetation like a boat with him helpless at the wheel.

1053

One of the worst automotive marketing own-goals was in 1994, when thousands of Spanish women received an anonymous printed letter in an unmarked envelope. Inside it read: "Yesterday we passed in the street and I saw you looking at me with interest. I only have to be with you a few minutes and . . . I promise you won't forget our experience together." None of the women knew who it was from until a follow-up letter arrived. This claimed to be from a car, the Fiat Cinquecento, and encouraged the recipient to test drive it. Instead, the stalking style of letter worried some women so much that they called the police. Fiat was taken to court and, despite its protests that it was harmless promotional campaign, was fined by the government. It was also forced to pay damages to one of the women.

1054

The Jaguar car company started off making side-cars for motorbikes.

1055 - 1058

Traffic cones were invented by American street painter Charles Scanlon in 1943. Scanlon was inspired while working on street sites in Los Angeles protected by makeshift wooden barriers. He patented an idea for a stacking, hollow cone... and it was so successful there are now an estimated 140 million traffic cones in use around the world.

- British engineer David Morgan is credited with the world's largest collection of traffic cones. Morgan has 137 covering what is believed to be every type of traffic cone ever made.
- The latest traffic cones can be made from recycled plastic bottles.

1059

The fastest ever diesel car was the BMW Alpina D5 S which had a top speed of 178mph (286kph).

1060

After Steve Davis from Derbyshire, England, suffered his second stroke he vowed it would not stop him fulfilling a childhood dream... to become a racing driver. As soon as he left hospital he bought a Ginette sports car, joined the British GT race series and formed an association to help stroke victims take part in motorsports.

1061

Felix Wankel, inventor of the Wankel rotary engine used in NSU and Mazda cars, couldn't drive and was a Senior Assault Unit Leader in the Nazi SS.

1062 - 1063

Argentine Juan Manuel Fangio was considered the best motor racing driver of all time because he won almost every other Grand Prix he entered: 24 wins in 51 Grand Prix. That winning rate has never been bettered.

- A mythical story was told by an American oilman involved in a road accident while Fangio's passenger. He said that they suddenly saw a truck that had stalled in the dark completely blocking the road ahead. Fangio deliberately spun his car to avoid hitting it. Fangio and his wife were thrown out. The indignant truck-driver shouted at the American: "Who do you think you are, driving like that? Fangio?" The American replied: "No, but he is," as he pointed to the injured Argentinian. The truck-driver stared in horror… and then burst into tears.

1064

China's largest SUV and pick-up truck manufacturer is based in Hebie, near the end of the Great Wall of China. So the company named itself Great Wall. Its logo? That's a graphic representation of part of the wall of course. It shows one of the towers along the wall.

1065 - 1070

A survey of motorists found that the most annoying driving habits in other drivers are:

1) Not indicating
2) Leaving full beam lights on
3) Driving 10mph below the speed limit
4) Tailgating
5) Last minute lane mergers

* Of those that voted in the survey, 87% also admitted doing at least one of the annoying habits themselves.

1071

A complex mathematical study by motor racing experts of points won, cars driven, competitors beaten and teams involved, attempted to find the best F1 drivers of the 21st century. The final verdict was:

10 Ralf Schumacher

9 Juan Pablo Montoya

8 Nico Rosberg

7 Max Verstappen

6 Jenson Button

5 Kimi Raikkonen

4 Fernando Alonso

3 Michael Schumacher

2 Sebastian Vettel

1 Lewis Hamilton

1072 - 1076

Indian manufacturer Hindustan built an ageing British saloon car… for 57 years. The Indian manufacturer bought the rights and tooling of the 1955 Morris Oxford from the British Motor Corporation. The spacious but elderly design was created by Alec Issigonis, who later designed the Mini.

Renamed the 'Ambassador' the car was launched in India in 1957 with a geriatric 1476cc side-valve engine that was later replaced by a slightly more modern 1950s overhead-valve B-Series engine.

The simple style of the Ambassador struck a chord with Indian buyers and the car dominated their motoring world for decades. Here are some trivia facts about it:

- By the 1980s it was so popular it represented more than two-thirds of the sub-continent's car production and had a waiting list of a year.
- Incredibly, the Ambassador remained in production until 2014.
- In 2013 the Ambassador was hailed as the best taxi car in the world by BBC Top Gear.

1077 - 1079

Blacksmith's son Soichiro Honda ran a workshop producing piston rings for Toyota until it was destroyed in the Second World War. So in 1946 he started making motorised bikes, which were so successful he founded his own Honda Motor Company. It did well. By 1964 he ran the world's biggest motorcycle manufacturer.

- Today the multinational Honda corporation is so big it has its own airport in Japan
- Company founder Soichiro Honda once said: "Success represents the 1% of your work which results from the 99% that is called failure"

1080 - 1098

Here are 18 marketing names for automatic gearboxes

> Alfa Romeo: Selespeed
> Audi: S-Tronic
> Ford: Cruise-o-matic, Powershift
> Edsel: Mile-o-matic
> Chrysler: TorqueCommand
> Mercedes: G-Tronic
> GM: Dynaflow, Powerglide, Turboglide, Whirlaway Hydra-Matic
> Holden: Trimatic
> Skoda/Seat: DSG
> Aston Martin: Touchtronic
> Fiat: Dualogic
> Lotus: IPS (Intelligent Precision Shift)
> MG: DCT
> Porsche: PDK
> Renault: EDC
> Subaru: Lineartronic
> Smart: Twinamic
> Citroen/Peugeot: EAT (Efficient Automatic Transmission)

1099 – 1105

A 2+2 car is a coupe with an extra two small seats in the back. Here are six examples:

> Jaguar E-Type 2+2
> Lotus Elan 2+2
> Nissan 300ZX 2+2
> Chevrolet Monza 2+2
> Mustang 2+2 (1965)
> Pontiac 2+2 (1964)

1106

The fastest ever production Jeep was the Jeep Grand Cherokee Trackhawk of 2017. The five-door SUV had 707bhp and could accelerate from 0-60mph in 3.5 seconds.

1107 – 1113

Six of the longest car names in history
(From carthrottle.com)

1 Land Rover Range Rover Evoque 2.0 TD4 E-Capability 4x4 HSE Dynamic
2 Lamborghini Aventador LP 750-4 Superveloce Roadster
3 Open Insignia Sports Tourer 2.0BTurbo CDTi ecoFlex
4 Mercedes-Benz R 300 CDI DPF BlueEfficiency 7G-Tronic
5 Alfa Romeo 6C 2300 B Lungo Cabriolet Posti Castagna
6 Alfa Romeo 159 Sportwagon ti JTS 16V Selespeed

1114

A billboard ad in California promoted the Audi 4 with a glamorous photo of the car and the cheeky slogan to its rival brand: 'Your move BMW.'

Local BMW dealers reacted by booking the billboard alongside, and designing a poster featuring the latest BMW 3-Series with the single word: "Checkmate".

1115 - 1117

In one of the automotive world's biggest marketing gaffes, in April 2013 Hyundai Motors released a TV commercial depicting a man trying to kill himself using the carbon monoxide exhaust fumes of a Hyundai ix35.

His suicide attempt fails however - because the Hyundai's fumes are so clean and non-toxic.

The advert, produced by Hyundai's in-house agency, received widespread criticism for promoting suicide and from people whose relatives had died in similar circumstances. Hyundai eventually took down the video and issued an apology.

- Skoda ran a magazine commercial in Ireland showing a groom on his wedding day weighing up three options: (a) keep her, (b) give her back to Daddy or (c) trade her in for her younger sister. The slogan said: Wouldn't it be nice if we all had these options?

- Ford was forced to fire an agency boss and publically apologise after an advert was used in India showing Italian leader Silvio Berlusconi using one of its cars to kidnap three young women. They were shown tied up and gagged in the luggage area of a Ford F-go along with the slogan 'Leave your worries behind – with F-go's extra-large boot'.

1118

A Hummer has up to 28 different warning lights on the dashboard.

1119

A short Japanese river is famed throughout the country because it flows through the grand Ise religious shrine. The river translates into English as "50 bells" and is so highly thought-of that a multi-national Japanese motor manufacturer named itself after the Isuzu River.

1120

In 1945 the Swallow Sidecar company decided to drop its name as the initials SS had become toxic through their use by extreme Nazis in the Second World War. So Britain's SS changed its name to Jaguar.

1121

American TV host Jay Leno now owns Steve McQueen's former Jaguar XKSS which the Hollywood star drove so fast that he earned two driving bans.

1122

A Nissan Leaf broke a British record in July 2020 by driving 230 miles from Nissan's technical centre in Cranfield, Bedfordshire, to the Nissan factory in Sunderland. It was fitted with radar and laser technology… but had no driver.

1123 - 1124

The 1999 Mitsubishi Pajero/Shogun SUV had the world's biggest ever four-cylinder production car engine at 3.2 litres. Mitsubishi also produced the highest-powered four-cylinder engine too. The 2.0-litre unit in the 2016 Lancer Evo produced a hefty 440bhp.

- At the time of writing Bugatti's Chiron has the world's largest production car engine at 8.0 litres.

1125

Californian car enthusiast Robert 'Woody' Woodill built his own sport car in 1950, using a Willy's jeep engine and axles, a custom-made steel frame and a body moulded in a new material: fibreglass. The light weight helped it to a 120mph (193kph) top speed.

A huge positive reaction from the public made Woodill build and sell another 15 of his Wildfire two-seaters – making it the first production car with a fibreglass body. The survivors are now rare collectors items and one sold in 2012... for more than $100,000 (£79,000).

1126 – 1151

Here are 25 of the most peculiar oddball cars ever built:
(From roadandtrack.com)

25 Ferrari FF – four-wheel-drive V12 estate
24 Toyota Sera – small family car with butterfly doors
23 Chevrolet SSR – convertible V8 sports pick-up truck
22 Nissan Pulsar NX – modular rear was interchangeable
between coupe or estate
21 GMC Envoy XUV – SUV with pick-up loadbay
20 BMW Z1 – peculiar shape, lights and doors
19 Lamborghini LM002 – ugly V12 super-SUV
18 Subaru Brat –pick-up with rear-facing seats in loadbay
17 Chysler Crossfire – weird mix of US and German design
16 Lincoln Blackwood – luxury pickup with prestige grille and
carpeted loadbay
15 Isuzu VehiCross – Mad-Max futuristic SUV
14 Toyota Previa – mid-engined people-carrier
13 Mercedes G63 AMG 6x6 – G-Wagon pick-up with
six-wheel drive
12 Fiat Multipla – 'the ugliest car ever made'
11 Alfa Romeo SZ – weird slabby coupe like a slice a cake
10 Citroen SM – half Citroen, half Maserati
9 Edsel Corsair – 'one of the biggest disasters in the history of
the automobile'
8 Helicron – 1930s French propeller-driven two-seater
7 Ferrari Berlinetta Boxer – Ferrari design that was 'a bit off'
6 Lancia Fulvia Sport Zagato – 'not traditionally beautiful'
5 Lotus Europa – 'left conventional standards of automotive
beauty at the door'
4 Plymouth Valiant – distinctive sixties cult classic
(Continues overleaf)

3 Renault Alpine GTA – weird plastic supercoupe

2 Stout Scarab – rear-engined V8 minivan looked like an insect

1 Subaru SVX – unique 90s futuristic window-within-a-window design disaster

1152

After the Second World War, victorious Russian forces took over the BMW factory in East Germany.

Under Soviet control the factory continued building its cars - but they were now labelled EMWs instead of BMWs, as they were from the city of Eisenacher not Bavaria where BMW had its headquarters.

The EMW badge was similar - but with a red and white 'propeller' motif instead of BMW's blue and white. After 1955 the EMW brand was dropped and the factory switched to making Wartburg cars.

1153

In 2020 the New South Wales government in Australia awarded a grant of almost $1million AUD (£550,000/US $700,000) to a local company to develop a flying car.

1154

The Volvo L331 was an exceptionally rugged off-road vehicle produced in the sixties. It was particularly popular with military purchasers around the world. No-one dared say anything at the time however, when the Saudi Arabian government bought 200 of them, all specified with racks on the roof… to hold skis.

1155 - 1156

The word coupe was first applied to horse-drawn carriages without rear-facing seats, as it was a shortened, truncated version of bigger more traditional carriages, hence the French word coupé or 'cut'.

- A berlinetta is a sports coupe, the word derives from the Italian word for 'little saloon'

1157 - 1164

Here are seven Hollywood Jeeps:

> M*A*S*H
> Jurassic Park
> Dukes of Hazzard (Daisy's Jeep)
> Cars (Sarge)
> Tomb Raider: Lara Croft
> Saving Private Ryan
> Band of Brothers

1165

After 14 years of development, the luxurious Bugatti Royale was launched in 1927. The three-tonne limousine had real ivory switches and gearknob, a sumptuous velvet interior and one of the biggest ever production-car engines – a 12.7-litre straight 8-cylinder. The Royale was intended to be the French rival to Rolls Royce as the world's finest car – but only six were built. Despite its name and lofty ambitions, none were ever owned by a member of any Royal family.

1166

Kia and Hyundai have company headquarters next door to each other in Seoul, South Korea.

1167 - 1178

A study by iSeeCars.com analysed 31 years' worth of data to find which car manufacturers had issued the most and the least vehicle recalls.

Best five (least recalls per 1,000 vehicles)
1 Porsche
2 Mercedes
3 Kia
4 Tesla
5 Mazda

Worst five
14 BMW
15 Hyundai
16 Honda
17 Chrysler
18 VW

• A study of the <u>severity</u> of the consequences of the recall problem showed that the car manufacturer with the least severe recalls was Volvo and the manufacturer with the most severe recalls was Tesla.

1179

A thorough study of 24 million US car sales found that the car most likely to be resold within its first year of ownership is the BMW 3 Series.

1180 - 1181

In 1994 a new car took the title of the fastest accelerating two-wheel drive car in the world from the Bugatti EB110 supercar (according to Guinness World Records). It was the little-known hand-built Vertigo two-seater from tiny specialist sportscar maker Gillet, which is based in the small town of Gembloux in Belgium.

• Vertigo owners included Prince Albert of Monaco and French singer Johnny Hallyday.

1182 - 1183

There was almost an Italian version of the Porsche 911. Turin design house Bertone was commissioned to produce a cabrio version in 1966. The 911 Roadster was built and looked nothing like any existing Porsche – more like an Alfa Spider. It was dramatically revealed on the Porsche stand at that year's Geneva Auto Show. Not a single show visitor placed an order. And even after a few months there was still not a single order for the bizarre car… so Porsche quietly pulled the plug on the whole project.

• The one and only Bertone 911 was sold at Pebble Beach Auction in 2018 for $1.4 million (£1.1m).

1184 - 1188

An American motoring organisation looked at data from several research surveys to tell US car buyers which are the most reliable European cars they could buy. They were:

1 Porsche 911

2 VW Passat

3 Porsche Panamera

4 Volvo XC70

1189 - 1200

A recent internet poll, conducted by Hyundai, aimed to find 'the greatest on-screen automotive iconic character'. It returned this result:

1 Jeremy Clarkson

2 Steve McQueen

3 Richard Hammond

4 Vin Diesel

5 Sean Connery

6 James May

7 Paul Walker

8 Daniel Craig

9 Roger Moore

10 Jason Statham

* James Bond's Aston Martin DB5 was named the greatest movie car, ahead of Chitty Chitty Bang Bang and the De Lorean from Back to the Future.

1201

Unlucky van driver Ben Baron from Lancashire, England, slowly drove past the speed camera where he had been caught previously in 2021.

This time he carefully kept under the limit but couldn't stop himself making a infamous rude gesture at the hated camera… with both hands at once.

Unfortunately for Ben his hands-off-the-wheel gestures were again caught on camera and he promptly received another prosecution by post, this time for "failing to keep proper control of his van".

1202

Simon Heptinstall is a writer based in Wiltshire, England. His previous books include The Car Miscellany, described by reviewers as 'crammed with fun facts', and Car Marques, which reviewers noted 'has a bright yellow cover'.

1203

Simon Heptinstall once drove a Hillman Avenger that he bought for £50 from Lands End to John OGroats to show it could be done in car costing less than the train fare - although the journey was interrupted halfway when he was rushed from Walsall motorway services to the nearest hospital by ambulance semi-conscious due to the effect of exhaust fumes pouring up through a hole in the floor.

1204

Simon Heptinstall once drove to 12 countries in 12 hours, setting a new world record. The countries were, in order: England, France, Belgium, the Netherlands, Luxemburg, Germany, Switzerland, Lichtenstein, Italy, Austria, Slovenia and Croatia. The car used was a BMW 740.